A View From Black Mesa

A View From Black Mesa

The Changing Face of Archaeology

GEORGE J. GUMERMAN

The University of Arizona Press

TUCSON & LONDON

About the Author

GEORGE J. GUMERMAN has been involved with the Black Mesa Archaeological Project since 1968. He directed the project for Prescott College in Arizona until moving it to Southern Illinois University at Carbondale where he has been professor of anthropology and director of the Center for Archaeological Investigations. Dr. Gumerman's major continuing research efforts are in the American Southwest and Micronesia in the far western Pacific. His special interest is coordinating large multidisciplinary projects involving reconstruction of past environments.

Title page photograph by Robert Layhe

Second printing 1992
The University of Arizona Press
Copyright © 1984
The Arizona Board of Regents
All Rights Reserved

This book was set in 10/12 Linotron Galliard.
Manufactured in the U.S.A.
♾ This book is printed on acid-free, archival-quality paper.

Library of Congress Cataloging in Publication Data

Gumerman, George J.
   A view from Black Mesa.

   Bibliography: p.
   Includes index.
   1. Indians of North America—Arizona—Black Mesa
(Navajo County and Apache County)—Antiquities.
2. Black Mesa (Navajo County and Apache County, Ariz.)—
Antiquities. 3. Excavations (Archaeology)—Arizona—
Black Mesa (Navajo County and Apache County) 4. Arizona
—Antiquities.   I. Title.
E78.A7G964   1984   979.1′35   84-8581

ISBN 0-8165-0848-8
ISBN 0-8165-1340-6 (pbk.)

To Essie, Wolf, and Liz

Contents

▧ FIGURES

Tables

Preface

SOUTHWESTERN ARCHAEOLOGY, indeed, archaeology throughout the United States, is changing at a colossal rate. Advances in technique, increases in the amount of work undertaken, and the resulting accelerated pace of discovery have been widely publicized.

Less well known is the changing sociology of modern archaeology—who does the work, why, how, and the effect personality has on the results of archaeological projects. This book attempts to elucidate not only the method and theory of contemporary archaeology, and its historical antecedents, but the sociology of archaeology as well.

The vehicle for understanding these changes is a great archaeological endeavor on Black Mesa on the Navajo and Hopi reservations in northeastern Arizona near Monument Valley. The fifteen-year-long, and still continuing, project provides a basis for understanding the revolutionary changes sweeping American archaeology.

The chronicle is in many ways a personal narrative for it is important to understand how an individual's academic training, personality, and biases affect the archaeological research. It is the meshing of personalities, individual research interests, skills, weaknesses, the state of archaeological art, and bureaucratic and logistical demands that shape any archaeological project.

No longer can the contemporary archaeologist afford the luxury of being intellectually responsible for all phases of a large project. In the past dynamic individuals could secure the funding, provide the intellectual thrust, organize the expedition, supervise all the assistants and laborers, and write the entire final report. These individuals depended on their own skills and did not have to worry about government supervisors, tribal governments, and university or museum bureaucracies. Today, as unfortunate graduate students soon learn, large-scale archaeology involves a broad array of specialists and requires a great deal of nonarchaeological activity. The principal investigator, if it is a single individual, must coordinate and orchestrate rather than dominate the intellectual thrust of the project.

This book describes the reshaping of the approach to archaeological research. The changes are not complete, and they never will be, nor have they been accomplished without some stretching and even tearing of the fabric of the organization of archaeology. The redefining of the methods, goals, and organizational structure of archaeology, the modifying and fine tuning of research designs, provides the tableau within which archaeological research results must be viewed.

This book is not meant as a definitive statement about research on Black Mesa. In many cases it has been necessary to generalize about specific research projects and to delete many of the qualifying statements which scientists find necessary to surround their work. In other instances ongoing research is modifying statements made in this volume, and new research endeavors have had to be left out. In sum, readers interested in the specifics of any individual study used as an example here must refer directly to that study.

ꕥ ACKNOWLEDGMENTS

This volume, a labor of love, was not accomplished without a great deal of assistance. I am especially grateful to the School of American Research where this book was written and its president

Douglas Schwartz and his friendly and helpful staff. Funds making my stay at the school as a resident scholar possible were provided by the National Endowment for the Humanities, Peabody Coal Company, and Southern Illinois University at Carbondale.

It is obviously impossible for me to thank the hundreds of individuals associated with the Black Mesa Archaeological Project. I hope that my blanket expression of gratitude conveys some sense of my deep appreciation to all of them. Peabody Coal Company officials deserve special thanks for putting up with something they never totally understood. Equally supportive were high-level Southern Illinois University officials, Lou Shelby, Worthen Hunsaker, Don Wilson, John Guyon, and Mike Dingerson, who often acted as seeing eye dogs through the blindness of bureaucratic red tape. Numerous individuals were of help in reviewing and commenting on this manuscript, especially Barbara E. Cohen, Robert Euler, Robert Layhe, William Lipe, Judy Machen, Gary Melvin, Shirley Powell, Joe Stevens, Gwinn Vivian, and John Ware. Most of the drawings were rendered by Dana Anderson. Photographs were taken by Robert Euler, Robert Dunlavey, Wolf Gumerman, Paul Long, John Richardson and John Ware.

GEORGE J. GUMERMAN

A View From Black Mesa

I

The Changing Face
of Archaeology

B LACK MESA LIES in the northeast corner of Arizona like
the upturned palm of a giant hand, fingers spreading to the
southwest. These fingers are the Hopi Mesas. On them perch
the ancient but still-inhabited villages of the Hopi Indians, without whose ancestors there would be no raw material for this book.

Under the sandstone cap and thin soil cover of Black Mesa lies
a thick layer of low-sulphur coal, the important energy source for
the urban Southwest and the object of intensive mining by the
Peabody Coal Company. Since 1967 Peabody has supported archaeological work on Black Mesa, demonstrating that there are
indirect, though ironic, benefits from surface mining. Results of
these archaeological investigations are not architecture and artifacts—crumbling walls, broken pots, corn-grinding implements,
and arrowheads—but technical reports which describe the behavior of prehistoric people who lived on Black Mesa.

This particular type of archaeology is generated by Indian tribal,
state, and federal statutes requiring that information be gathered
before it is lost to the bulldozer's blade or the rising waters of a
dam, and that it become part of the public record. While the gathering of such data is supported by public policy, public trust, and
in most instances public monies, the public itself has benefited

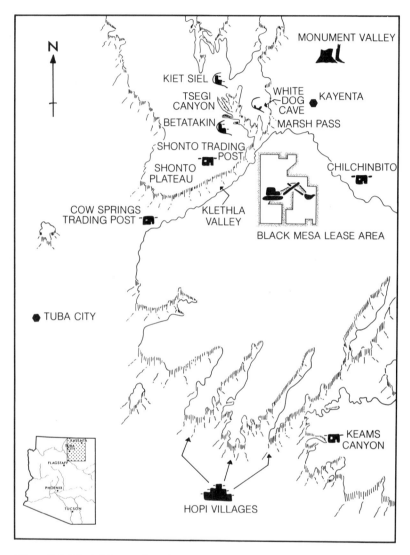

Figure 1.1. Black Mesa and environs

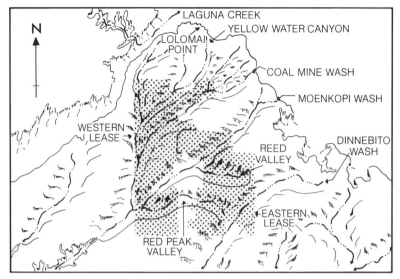

Figure 1.2. The northeastern part of Black Mesa showing Peabody Coal Company's lease area

little except in the very general sense that human knowledge has increased. Virtually no laymen and relatively few professionals have read the highly technical, statistic-filled reports.

This book endeavors to make the substance of one important archaeological project accessible to the general reader. The writing of such a book is based on a conviction that modern archaeology's true goal is not the spectacular find, but increased understanding of human behavior in the past and appreciation for its influence on our own lives.

The Black Mesa Archaeological Project (BMAP) provides a good vehicle for making the archaeologist's work more accessible and for examining the changing face of southwestern archaeology.

The project area encompasses 64,858 acres of the Navajo and Hopi Indian reservations on the northeastern portion of Black Mesa, an area leased to the Peabody Coal Company for mining (Figs. 1.1 and 1.2). The prehistoric people who lived in this harsh but beautiful environment were the Anasazi, the ancestors of the modern Pueblo Indians.

Black Mesa was not a major Anasazi population center, although it was situated in the heart of Anasazi country. Cliff dwellings like those found at Navajo National Monument and Mesa Verde, and large prehistoric towns such as Chaco Canyon in New Mexico, were absent. Nor was Black Mesa a focal point for trade or Anasazi culture innovation. Instead, the prehistoric people of Black Mesa were simple farmers living in small groups spread out over the rugged, piñon- and juniper-studded landscape, scratching a living out of the arid soil.

The spartan lifestyle and relative material poverty of these people would seem to make Black Mesa an unpromising and certainly unexciting area in which to conduct archaeology. But, it is precisely because of the paucity of spectacular remains that Black Mesa is a unique natural and cultural laboratory for understanding Anasazi behavior. The majority of the Anasazi did not live in the grandiose cliff dwellings or hugh trade-oriented towns, but in rural areas like Black Mesa (Fig. 1.3). They produced and consumed few luxury goods and left very few things that impress the modern eye. Yet they played a vital role in a complex social and economic system.

The large Anasazi population centers cannot be understood fully without understanding the broad network of smaller communities such as those on Black Mesa. The reverse is also true, for

Figure 1.3. The northeastern edge of Black Mesa

the thousands of small farming settlements were often profoundly affected by the larger towns.

The social and economic system that linked these communities of vastly different scale is only now being investigated and understood. In the past, archaeologists concentrated their efforts on large individual sites. Now it is the network of sites that is the major focus of most archaeological investigations. This broadening of focus reflects a philosophical and methodological shift in archaeology that has occurred in recent years. The Black Mesa Archaeological Project has been in the forefront of this movement.

But before examining BMAP in detail, it is necessary to place it in perspective—to learn something of southwestern archaeology and archaeologists, past and present.

⚘ ARCHAEOLOGY: MYTH AND REALITY

Alfred Vincent Kidder, dean of southwestern archaeologists, once wrote that "In popular belief, and unfortunately to some extent in fact, there are two sorts of archaeologists, the hairy-chested and the hairy-chinned." He described the hairy-chested archaeologist as "a strong-jawed young man in a tropical helmet, pistol on hip, hacking his way through the jungle in search of lost cities and buried treasure."

The hairy-chinned archaeologist on the other hand was "old" and "benevolently absent-minded. His only weapon is a magnifying glass, with which he scrutinizes inscriptions in forgotten languages. Usually his triumphant decipherment coincides . . . with [his] daughter's rescue from savages by the handsome young assistant."

Kidder was amused by these stereotypes because he knew as well as anyone the reality that lay behind the Saturday matinee facade. Son of a mining engineer and a graduate of Harvard, he made his first archaeological foray into the Southwest in 1907. From 1915 to 1929, he and his colleagues toiled at a large site called Pecos Ruin, a few miles east of Santa Fe, New Mexico. This project, and other smaller projects in which Kidder participated in Arizona, Utah, and New Mexico, resulted in the first systematic synthesis of southwestern archaeology; it provided a framework for understanding the evolution of prehistoric southwestern culture which is still used today. Kidder's genius for observing regularities in the archaeological record brought order out of the chaos that passed for southwestern archaeology at that time.

In 1928 Harold S. Gladwin, a former Pennsylvania coal miner, Montana cow puncher, and Wall Street stock broker, began excavating a large ruin called Gila Pueblo in Six Shooter Canyon near Globe, Arizona, reconstructing the rooms as he went. The rebuilt site, complete with its tiny rooms, became the home of a private archaeological research foundation known as Gila Pueblo. This foundation was an intellectual center for southwestern archaeology during the 1930s and 1940s. Along with his colleague, Emil W. Haury, Gladwin identified and described two of the three major southwestern prehistoric cultures: the Hohokam of southern Arizona and the Mogollon of the central mountains of Arizona and New Mexico. Haury, who has long been the dominant figure in southwestern archaeology, fondly recalls those glorious years full of vigorous late-night discussions about archaeology followed by impetuous rushes to various parts of the Southwest to field test the ideas that were germinated.

Archaeologist Paul S. Martin, working out of the Field Museum of Natural History at the University of Chicago, came to the Southwest in the early 1930s. He is best remembered for the archaeology field school he ran in the White Mountains of Arizona in the 1960s and 1970s. He and the bright young students who were attracted to him changed the thrust of southwestern archaeology from largely descriptive research to attempts at discovering the regularities of past human behavior. His students are now at universities throughout the United States carrying on his tradition of creative thinking about the past.

While the backgrounds and careers of these archaeologists differed in many ways, they did have two things in common: formidable intellect and an insatiable curiosity about the past. Their visceral hunger for knowledge and their love of their work made them giants in the field. These men, not the hairy-chested or hairy-chinned caricatures, should provide the public with its image of the archaeologist and students with their role model. They were the real thing—scholars worthy of emulation.

The path blazed by these archaeological pioneers has, however, taken a sharp turn in recent years. This turn has been caused by the infusion into the profession of huge, previously undreamed of sums of money and the corresponding development of a new type of archaeology and archaeologist.

CONTRACT ARCHAEOLOGY

The growth of the environmental and historical preservation movements in the 1960s led to a heightened concern for the conservation of America's natural and cultural resources. Many archaeologists shared this concern. They realized that rapid population growth and a rise in construction activity were threatening the archaeological record. Entire data bases for the study of past cultures and periods already had been lost.

In the late 1960s and early 1970s, federal, state, and local laws were passed requiring the study of archaeological remains in danger of destruction by earth-moving activities. These laws opened the flood gates of funding, pumping millions of dollars into what is now known as contract archaeology, that is archaeology underwritten by companies or government agencies undertaking work which endangers sites.

Coinciding with this legal and financial upheaval was an intellectual revolution in American archaeology. Many young scholars began to reexamine their goals and methods, feeling that an understanding of who lived where and when was not the ultimate objective of archaeology. They believed it was necessary to understand why and how cultures change. Their new goal was not simply to understand change within a single culture, but rather change in terms of universal human behavior.

Old-style questions such as "What effect did decreasing annual rainfall have on the people of Black Mesa in the twelfth century?" were rephrased to ask "How can an understanding of the effects of decreasing annual rainfall on prehistoric Black Mesa help explain the behavior of any mixed agriculture and hunting-and-gathering society in a semi-arid environment?" In other words, archaeologists began urging one another to be social scientists as well as prehistorians.

This shift in emphasis continues today as archaeologists strive to understand culture as a total system. Archaeology is no longer the detached study of potsherds and architectural styles; instead it is the study of social, economic, and even religious systems whose interaction constitutes culture. Artifacts and architecture are simply manifestations of these subsystems.

The archaeological approach that focuses on the interrelationships of cultural subsystems and the environment is known as cultural ecology or the ecosystem approach. To successfully employ this approach it is necessary to examine an environment and ways people adapt to it. In archaeological theory, environment is considered not only natural surroundings, but also other cultures in direct or indirect contact with the culture under study.

The ecosystem approach provides a view of the totality of culture. However it is a static view, a slice of prehistoric life at a particular time and in a specific place. The concept of evolution must be injected into the system to make it dynamic and to explain change.

Cultural systems are continually evolving, adapting to their natural and social environment in a process called cultural evolution. In many ways cultural evolution is analogous to biological evolution. Some cultures are able to adapt better and more quickly than others, and this adaptability may vary at different times and under different conditions.

The study of cultural ecology and cultural evolution demands new methods. In the past, archaeologists were content to describe the archaeological record and infer past behavior from it. Now they attempt to prove rather than to infer, which demands a new methodological rigor and more precise use of the scientific method. Archaeological data are now subject to rigorous testing, quantification, and scientific analysis. Increasingly, they are manipulated by computers.

Another necessary change has been the employment of specialists from a wide variety of disciplines to focus on a single problem. If archaeologists look at culture as an adaptive system reacting to its natural environment, they must understand in considerable detail what that environment was. No large archaeological project can do without the input of botanists, zoologists, geologists, and a host of other natural scientists who help reconstruct past climates and plant and animal populations.

While these new directions in archaeological research appear sound, their implementation is exceedingly difficult. It has been necessary to devise a new organizational structure to support large, long-term, multidisciplinary team research projects.

The era of the lone scholar in archaeology is gone. The kinds of questions archaeologists are now asking about patterns of human behavior require a team approach. This change in organizational structure demands a complementary change in funding structure. Archaeology has always been expensive, but team research and new technical procedures have made the costs staggering.

Fortunately, the emergence and growth of contract archaeology has coincided with development of the new research goals and methods. Contract dollars have enabled archaeologists to address broad research concerns and utilize techniques that otherwise would be prohibitively expensive for private or public foundations. Contract archaeology has provided many young archaeologists with meaningful employment and also has led to the excavation of a more representative sample of sites used by various prehistoric groups. Instead of just big habitation sites, small hunting camps and burial sites are investigated. This gives a broader more realistic picture of a culture.

Seemingly something close to an archaeological utopia has been created, but sadly this is not the case. Serious problems exist, many of which can be directly or indirectly attributed to the infusion on a national level of over $100 million annually into archaeological efforts.

The "bottom-line" always has been an important, though often unstated factor in archaeological research. The professional who did high quality archaeology and produced superior publications usually was rewarded with an above-average salary, extra travel support for attending professional meetings, and consulting fees denied less productive archaeologists.

The gusher of contract dollars has raised the stakes. For a young archaeologist, success at securing a large contract project can make the difference between rapid career advancement and professional stagnation. The archaeologist's supporting institution also has a strong interest. Students are attracted by jobs generated by such projects, and administrative overhead charges tacked onto a contract can provide a financial cushion in an era of shrinking budgets.

Abuses of high overhead charges are not uncommon; one comprehensive museum and research institution in the Southwest gets 80 percent of its operating budget from archaeological contract overhead charges. Many other institutions both inside and outside academia are dependent on "soft money," funds brought in by contract jobs.

The message for many archaeologists is clear: secure contracts or else. The pressure is intensified by the process of competitive bidding. It is not unusual to have six or seven institutions and firms bidding for a single contract. For some archaeologists the temptation to cut costs and bid low to obtain a contract and preserve their jobs is overwhelming. This situation can, and sometimes has, produced disastrous consequences for archaeology—reports not published, curation of artifacts ignored, or less site excavation than is warranted. This is tragic, for the lifeblood of all scholarly activity is shared research results. Failure to share archaeological results is doubly deplorable because, unlike research in physics or chemistry, archaeological research cannot be replicated. A site, once excavated, is gone. The artifacts themselves, without a detailed description of their relationship to one another and to the site's architecture and environment, lose much of their meaning.

When reports *are* published they are too often filled with incomprehensible technical jargon or are solely descriptive, devoid of any evidence of creative thinking. Such reports comply with the letter but not the spirit of the law.

Allied against these abuses and potential abuses are various government agencies manned by a new breed of archaeo-bureaucrat. Many of these individuals are not called archaeologists, but rather by the awkward title of "cultural resource managers." Their job, an essential one, is to ensure that the laws preserving antiquities are followed. They help archaeologists assess the value of sites, make sure that surveys and excavations are done properly, and perform other, often thankless, tasks.

Like archaeologists, cultural resource managers come in a wide range of competencies. Working for different agencies, and with different interpretations of the statutes, they have produced a welter of conflicting requirements for the archaeologist and his client. Often, different district offices of the same agency require different kinds of archaeological tasks.

Much of the confusion is due to the newness of the legislation and the cultural resource managers' and archaeologists' inexperience in dealing with regulations and policy; but there are some signs that order is being imposed. However, the hope is that situations never become so overorganized that it is necessary to do archaeology by a set formula. In some instances this has happened. Federal employees have demanded items in contracts that call for the number of trenches to be excavated and their length and width. No archaeologist can be hamstrung by requirements such as these and still perform creative research archaeology. If what lay beneath the surface was so well known that the precise techniques used to excavate could be ordained beforehand, there would be no need to excavate. Unfortunately, rigid requirements have been built into contracts in response to abuses by archaeologists, who have sometimes done little work for their money or used inappropriate techniques.

Offending contractors and cultural resource managers are a minority and have not replaced the archaeologists who are concerned with both protecting the resource base and understanding past human behavior. However, their shoddy practices are creating a damaging new image of archaeology in the mind of the public. Reports of Alaskan firms vying for Arizona contracts, lawsuits between archaeological contractors, and archaeology-related delays in important construction projects now appear frequently in the press. Such negative publicity invites a backlash against all archaeologists, both good and bad. As we shall see, the impression the public gets from these newspaper accounts misses the mark as greatly as did the hairy-chinned and hairy-chested myths of yore.

The laws, the funding, and the changing philosophy of conservation are essential for this archaeological generation. But change has swept down on the profession so fast that many mistakes have been made, and it will take some time to sort out and correct these mistakes. Most archaeologists are convinced that in time this can be done.

This saga is precisely about such a sorting out. It is the chronicle of a marriage between the world's largest coal company and an archaeological research project. Like all marriages it had its ups and downs. Unlike many marriages, it got better over the years.

2

A Short History of Anasazi Archaeology

NASAZI COUNTRY has always attracted the romantics. It was into this arid and rugged environment that the earliest southwestern archaeological investigators wandered. Their names are prominent in the pantheon of southwestern archaeology—Wetherill, Mindeleff, Cushing, and Fewkes. They had varied goals, but all shared a romantic nature and a burning curiosity about the past and the relationship of the ever-present ruins to the living indigenous people. They rode awestruck through lonely canyons in whose crevices were tucked large prehistoric "apartment houses," often with whole vessels, corn, and sandals still in place, almost as if the people had gone to work for the day and never returned.

Eastern philanthropists, eager to experience vicariously the isolation, spectacular scenery, encounters with living Indians, and thrill of discovery, financed many of these expeditions. As a result, crates of exquisite artifacts were shipped back to fill museum cases and wealthy individuals' private homes. The U.S. government also financed some archaeology, and in other instances expeditions were not supported but supporting—the artifacts recovered by private entrepreneurs were sold and archaeology became, for some, a lucrative business.

These early explorations did produce information of scholarly value, primarily detailed descriptions of artifacts and architecture and attempts to relate the prehistoric people to their descendants, the living Indians. Some of the large volumes of description of old Pueblo architecture, for example, were very detailed and accurate, and are now important historical documents.

The efforts to connect the prehistoric past and the historic present relied on Indian legends and oral history. Because of the great number of often conflicting legends and the inability of the early investigators to date the prehistoric ruins, these attempts were largely unsuccessful. When excavation was undertaken it was almost always at large, impressive-looking ruins where the chance of recovering sumptuous artifacts was high. This was often done to impress the expedition sponsor, be it a museum or an individual. Sites tended to be excavated for things, not information.

What these early adventurers were *not* concerned with particularly were questions of age or geographical extent. To be certain, there was musing about when sites might have been occupied and some discussion about the geographical distribution of certain artifactual and architectural traits, but for the most part these questions were ignored because it was believed that they could not be successfully addressed.

In the 1920s, 1930s, and 1940s, Kidder and many of his colleagues proved the early archaeologists wrong. The major concerns became chronology and the differences among cultural remains spread out over the landscape. Understanding local and temporal distribution demanded some scheme of classification, for only by recognizing similarities and differences could relationships be understood. A classification system was developed which allowed the pigeon-holing of artifact types, architecture, and whole prehistoric cultures into definable, easily distinguishable units. The stage was set for the development of a spatial and temporal framework for southwestern archaeology.

Dating was first accomplished in relative terms. No calendrical dates could be assigned, but artifacts or sites could be said to be older or younger than other artifacts or sites. The two methods for assigning relative dates were stratigraphy and the identification of artifact and dwelling styles on an evolutionary scale. These methods are described in detail in Chapter 4.

The ability to date artifacts in a calendrical sense was obtained in the late 1920s. A.E. Douglass, an astronomer at the University of Arizona, and his archaeological colleagues devised a chronology based on the annual growth rings in trees, which permitted the dating of wood samples to a specific year. After World War II, radiocarbon dating was developed. It also became important to archaeologists, but never in the Southwest to the extent that the much less expensive and more accurate tree-ring dating method did.

As southwestern archaeologists gained the ability to date sites and artifacts, they were able to distinguish between contemporaneous, yet geographically distinct cultural variations within Anasazi country. These local variations, comparable to differences between West Coast, midwestern, and East Coast American cultural styles today, were apparent in details of ceramics, architecture, and community size and configuration.

This ability to distinguish different temporal periods and different contemporaneous local cultural variations led to the development of an evolutionary scheme first articulated at the Pecos Conference, held at the pueblo ruin of Pecos in 1927. Here the Anasazi cultural continuum was divided into the Basketmaker and Pueblo periods, and then subdivided into Basketmaker I, II, and III, and Pueblo I through IV. This scheme is known as the Pecos Classification. Other classification schemes have since replaced it for research purposes, but the Pecos stages still provide a convenient framework for discussion, as we shall see in Chapter 5.

The archaeology of the 1940s, 1950s, and 1960s was a period of trying to "fill in the gaps" of the spatial and temporal framework that evolved earlier. Archaeologists were concerned with refining the chronology and determining how the valley or mesa where they were working could be fitted into the Pecos Classification and how a cultural assignment could be made based on regional differences. It was an unexciting time for southwestern archaeology. Although new ideas were not prominent, most sciences have to go through a stage of classification and data collecting before they can advance to the stage of developing and testing hypotheses.

By the late 1960s the ferment and excitement of the "new" archaeology took root and the course of modern southwestern archaeology was established. It was against this background that the Black Mesa Archaeological Project began.

3

Archaeologists, Businessmen, and Bureaucrats

A T THE 1967 PECOS CONFERENCE, an informal association of southwestern archaeologists, Bob Euler, then a faculty member at the spanking new Prescott College in Prescott, Arizona, pulled me aside and asked me if I would like to become involved in an archaeological project on Black Mesa. Peabody Coal Company had asked him to do an initial survey of part of their lease area and the right-of-way for a pipeline that would carry a coal-and-water mixture from their mine to power plants in Nevada, some 275 miles away (Fig. 3.1).

In those days many of us still believed that it was vitally important to fill in a gap on the archaeological map simply because "it was there." Black Mesa was intriguing because of its immense size, its location in the heart of Anasazi country, and the fact that it had been investigated by archaeologists just once, in 1936, the year I was born. Because of these factors, archaeologists had suggested for years that Black Mesa sites might provide answers to many questions raised by investigations in surrounding areas.

When Bob Euler confronted me, I was an advanced graduate student finishing my doctorate at the University of Arizona. Bob was looking for an archaeologist, still in his salad days, to teach at

Figure 3.1. Peabody Coal Company's surface mine on northern edge of Black Mesa

Prescott College and run a summer field school training students in the setting of a Black Mesa contract dig.

It was not the first time someone had asked me to work on Black Mesa. In 1966 I had accepted a fellowship at the Museum of Northern Arizona in Flagstaff, which gave me the opportunity to become involved in contract archaeology and get to know Anasazi archaeology by observing, digging, and analyzing.

During my tenure at the museum, Peabody Coal Company negotiated its lease with the Navajo and Hopi tribes to mine coal on Black Mesa and began drilling test holes and bulldozing roads. Not until after the leases were signed was Peabody informed that it would be responsible, under federal antiquity laws, for financing the recovery and analysis of archaeological remains. The company was referred to Ned Danson, director of the Museum of Northern Arizona, who briefed them on the requirements of contract archaeology. Ned then asked me to do a day's reconnaissance on Black Mesa to get some inkling of the archaeology and to see if Peabody's initial work had done much damage. After driving around with a Peabody engineer for a few hours, I concluded that the sites were small and that some of them had been damaged by test drilling. Shortly after reporting to Ned, I went back to the University of Arizona to write my dissertation.

Now, exactly one year later, Bob Euler was asking me to apply for the Prescott College and Black Mesa position. After the interview, Bob showed me the budget he was submitting to Peabody for the next summer's work. I was horrified, thinking Peabody would be scared off by what seemed to me an astronomical sum— over $30,000. But they agreed to it, and we began to prepare for the 1968 field season.

We had much to learn about archaeology as big business, and Peabody had a lot to learn about dealing with people trained in a scholarly tradition. In later years, for example, we could not understand why they kept changing the areas they wanted us to work in (additional drilling gave added information about coal quality and depth and the increasing price of coal made it more desirable to mine these areas).

They could not adequately evaluate our budgets. We should not have expected a Peabody vice president, trained as an engineer, to know how much it would cost to dig a village site. In desperation, because they were trying to defer costs until some coal was sold, they repeatedly questioned the small employee benefits, something they could understand. At times we would look at one another with stares of incomprehension.

A major source of misunderstanding on the part of both parties was due to the differences between large business's hierarchical structure (and to us, slavish obedience to "the boss") and the academic structure of collegiality (which to them seemed like anarchy). For example, a high-level professional archaeologist on the staff wrote a sympathetic but ill-advised letter to a local Navajo which could have resulted in major problems for Peabody. Somehow the letter reached an important Peabody official who demanded that the archaeologist, who also taught courses, be fired. As I pondered the dilemma of academic freedom versus propriety, the offending individual took a teaching position elsewhere. This permitted us, with only a slight guilty blush, to go back to the Peabody official and say "I fired him!"

Peabody certainly had difficulty understanding the imprecision of archaeology in particular and the wishy-washiness of academics in general. Most of the Peabody personnel we dealt with are engineers who, if given the task of, say, building a bridge, can pull a book off the shelf which gives formulae for the weight of certain bridge spans and the tensile strength of certain types of steel. Archaeologists on the other hand are more apt to respond to questions of how long will it take to dig a site with "if . . . maybe . . . I would guess," and the old standby, "if we knew what was there we wouldn't have to dig!"

After one frustrating contract negotiation, I called to say hello to our contact at Peabody Coal Company in St. Louis while I was there attending a national archaeological meeting. His response, delivered with a laugh, was "You mean I could get rid of all of you goddamn archaeologists by blowing up only one hotel!" I don't blame him; we must have been an incredible thorn in his side.

Over the years the relationship grew into one of greater understanding and mutual trust. It was simply a matter of time before we learned to appreciate each other's needs. It would have been different if Peabody had been vehemently antienvironmentalist, and we had been totally impractical ivory-tower academics.

Crucial to any archaeological field program is the support of the home base, be it an academic institution, research foundation, or museum. Office and laboratory space, accounting and billing services, and equipment such as typewriters and cameras are all part of the necessary support system. During the early years of BMAP, these were supplied by Prescott College; in return we trained students and the college received a percentage of the total contract for its administrative costs. While the accounting and billing procedures of the college left much to be desired, and in fact presaged its eventual bankruptcy, the other support services were more than adequate and we were well prepared for our first full field season.

At present our institutional home base is the bureaucratic behemoth of Southern Illinois University whose rules, regulations, and minds of petty officialdom were not devised for or attuned to the needs of a distant large archaeological project. For example, an internal audit showed that out of a budget of approximately one million dollars, we had misspent some thirty-odd dollars by giving away five T-shirts with the project's logo to employees. Misspent how? By reimbursing state employees outside normal salary channels! Fortunately university administrators higher up the ladder are more understanding and supportive, and after the archaeologists have expended all patience and much psychic energy, come to the rescue and smooth matters over.

✺ "BUZZ-WORMS" AND BLACK GNATS

When we arrived on Black Mesa that summer of 1968, the terrain was in almost pristine condition. Peabody had not yet begun to mine—they had not even improved the "road" which consisted of two muddy tire tracks.

We camped on a rocky, juniper-clad knoll, our bivouac consisting of two buildings, one for cooking and one for dining (Figs. 3.2 and 3.3). They were made so that the walls could be unbolted and the buildings moved to a new location. Students and staff slept in tents, electricity was provided by an ancient generator,

Figure 3.2. The first Black Mesa Archaeological Project camp in 1968

Figure 3.3. The heart of the project, the cookshed

and water was hand pumped from a well many miles away and hauled to the camp in a 500-gallon round tank on a flatbed trailer.

Mother nature was not kind to us. We soon discovered that our picturesque knoll sheltered a rattlesnake den. By the end of the summer we were quite blasé about dispatching them with a shovel, kept handy for the purpose, and had counted coup on some thirty "buzz-worms."

More feared by far than the rattlesnakes were the tiny but voracious black gnats. A few allergic people suffered swollen eyes and arms. More common is a simple maddening itch. My wife, a nurse, arrived on Black Mesa a few weeks after the start of the 1968 field season. She announced the worst thing to do for gnat bites was to scratch them. A few nights later I was awakened by her dragging the zipper of her sleeping bag over her bites. Nothing perhaps indicates the wondrous appetite of black gnats for human flesh than to see a woman wrapped in mosquito netting and smoking two cigars simultaneously in a futile effort at camouflage and smoke screen.

Considering the logistical and organizational challenge, the untrained crew, relatively inexperienced staff, and natural hazards, the archaeological work completed during the summer of 1968 was quite satisfactory. Our primary concern was determining the character of the archaeology: what types of sites were present, how old they were, and so on. The difficulties we encountered were due to an attempt to accomplish too much with too small a supervisory staff and inexperienced students. Supervisors had to spend time with logistical matters and the maintenance of equipment, time that should have been devoted to research concerns. Furthermore, the demands of conducting an archaeological field school were not entirely compatible with achieving research goals because so much time had to be spent training students.

The human problems were more vexing. In the course of any long-term project, a feeling of malaise inevitably sets in. Peoples' quirks are magnified, and camp fever becomes a virulent disease. This is a natural consequence of isolation, primitive living conditions, and sharing close quarters. At the end of the day you eat dinner, play volleyball, work in the lab, and share a tent with someone who may be your best friend or worst enemy. There is no escape.

For the project directors, these feelings intensify over the course of several field seasons. It is not the personnel problems which are most troublesome (although they are aggravating); rather, it is the difficulty in approaching research questions in a fresh and creative way. No matter how one tries, the creative juices dry up from too much field work and not enough contemplation. The dawn-until-dusk, seven-day-a-week job of director exhausts one. It is as simple as that.

Maintaining consistency in our research efforts on Black Mesa was also complicated by the financial instability of Prescott College. In 1973 Bob Euler moved to Ft. Lewis College in Durango, Colorado, taking BMAP with him, and I left for Southern Illinois University (SIU). The following December, Prescott declared bankruptcy and closed its doors.

In 1974 Bob became a federal employee, the research anthropologist at Grand Canyon National Park, and therefore had to give up the project. After much soul searching, I agreed to move the project to SIU on the condition that we could find a fulltime director. I was committed to the chairmanship of the anthropology department and could not give the project the time and attention it deserved. Besides, the project needed new intellectual blood. Bob and I had been too close to it too long. I selected a young doctoral candidate from the University of Michigan, Steve Plog. Steve had been raised in the pure tradition of the new archaeology and was more quantitatively oriented than either Euler or I. He took over with a firm hand, and the result was a new direction for BMAP.

Such a change in course is natural. Every archaeological project takes on its own personality, a personality dictated not only by the nature of the data, but by the interests, training, and personality of the archaeologist in charge. Since there are no basic archaeological "truths" to be discovered in any particular area, and the number of questions that can be addressed are almost infinite, the selection of the major research direction can often be a matter of chance.

Due to my academic training, my earlier work south of Black Mesa, and the influence of my friends and colleagues in the natural sciences, I was interested primarily in delineating Black Mesa's cultural history and explaining changes brought about by population increases and climatic fluctuations. Steve Plog's interests focused more on shifting patterns of food production and collection and trade so he instigated those types of studies on Black Mesa. He also led students into doing more refined studies of population changes.

Steve stayed with BMAP until 1978 when he accepted a position at the University of Virginia. He was replaced by Shirley Powell, an Arizona State University doctoral student who continued the process of refocusing and fine-tuning the research design, as well as refining the record-keeping required by increasing governmental and university regulations.

This shifting might appear to be disruptive, but those of us involved with BMAP found that change in personnel and the research design is inevitable and desirable. No individual, however intellectually and physically tireless, can stand the pace of running a large project year after year without becoming stale. Profound reasoning and brilliant insight are not everyday occurrences when faced with budget problems, hiring cooks, and leasing vehicles.

Then too, there is the need for fresh thinking to revitalize the research design with new methods and new ideas. It is crucial, however, that new researchers not drop old and still largely unanswered questions; instead they should build on them so that the project's scholarly direction evolves gradually and logically.

✒ HOW BMAP WORKS

Like other large projects, BMAP has evolved into a seasonal round of activity, with archaeologists moving with the sun, doing different tasks in different areas, from southern Illinois to northeastern Arizona. The ultimate goal of the yearly round of activity is different for each of the three parties involved: the coal company, the federal and state agencies, and the archaeologists. For Peabody Coal Company, the goal is to comply with the laws as effectively as possible to get on with the business of mining coal and making profits.

For the National Park Service and other government agencies, the goal is ensuring coal company compliance with the pertinent statutes and requiring archaeologists to carry out creative research which results in publication. As middlemen between the coal company and BMAP, the agencies must act impartially, helping the archaeologists maintain a solid research stance and the coal company obtain clearance to mine.

For the archaeologist, the ultimate goal is understanding the past. The scientific backdrop for all this activity is provided by the research design. The research design explains in great detail what kinds of problems are important and how to solve those problems. Since the research design is constantly evolving, each year produces not a new approach, but one which is slightly modified as a result of analysis and interpretation of the preceding year's data and evolution of archaeological method and theory.

The first part of the yearly cycle is most pleasurable, since it involves field work and archaeological survey. If Peabody needs clearance to mine a particular area, the region is systematically looked at to see if there are any archaeological remains. The results of the survey are then compiled and submitted to the

National Park Service. At a minimum, this includes a legal description of the sites, a map, a description of the surface features of each site including a summary of the artifacts on the surface, photographs of the site, and photographs and a general description of the environment.

BMAP evaluates the significance of the remains in order to recommend whether the sites are eligible for inclusion on the National Register of Historic Places. This step is important because, in the case of Black Mesa, only those sites determined eligible for the National Register can be excavated. Determining what sites are significant according to National Register guidelines is difficult because the guidelines recognize many kinds of significance. Ethnic significance depends on religious, mythological, or social importance to a specific subpopulation. The Hopis, for example, have religious shrines on Black Mesa. Public significance is based on aesthetic or educational value, such as the spectacular cliff dwellings of Mesa Verde. Scientific significance is most important to BMAP because that is what qualifies most of the Black Mesa sites. Sites on Black Mesa are determined to be significant if they appear to have the data potential necessary for answering questions posed in the BMAP research design. Sites which seem to have a long period of occupation, early sites, late sites, and sites with potential for providing information about past environments and subsistence techniques are especially appealing to BMAP archaeologists. Each site's data potential is evaluated against the research design which has been submitted and approved by the government agencies.

The National Park Service personnel then confer about the sites and the research design with the Arizona State Historic Preservation Officer (SHPO). The SHPO is responsible for establishing a record of significant sites within the state and making recommendations for sites to be placed on the National Register.

If the SHPO agrees with BMAP's recommendations, the National Park Service prepares very detailed documentation about the sites which is sent to the Bureau of Indian Affairs, the Navajo and Hopi tribes, and the U.S. Department of the Interior's Office of Surface Mining in Denver for approval. If approved, the National Park Service sends the documentation back to the SHPO, who then forwards it to Washington. There the documentation is evaluated by the National Heritage, Conservation and Recreation

Service, and if everything is acceptable, the sites are determined eligible for the National Register. They are not actually placed on the Register, just "determined eligible" for it; this permits their scientific study and eventual destruction. Peabody Coal Company is, at this point, legally responsible for excavating those sites.

Of course, what I have described is an ideal situation only approximated by reality. Recently the entire process has gotten more complicated because of "turf" disputes between federal agencies. The Office of Surface Mining revised almost all procedures, resulting in a nightmare of paperwork. There seems to be a direct correlation between attempts to scale down the federal work force and the amount of meddling the project gets. In one year BMAP's permit to excavate was granted two weeks before the close of the season. The Hopis required us to hire 100 percent Hopis as laborers and the Navajos required 100 percent Navajos! When necessary we just continue to operate, ignoring conflicting or unreasonable requirements, trying to do the best we can to comply with all the laws we know about. At times the director's job is mostly that of a negotiator or expediter.

The compliance process takes a great deal of time and is begun immediately after returning from the field in the fall. Because of the long waiting period, the archaeologists must assume that the research plan and documentation will be accepted and begin working with Peabody Coal Company on the excavation plan, budget, and contract for the following year. In most cases, only minor modification of the plan or site documentation is necessary. At the same time, permits for further archaeological work are requested from the Department of the Interior, the Navajo Tribe, and the Hopi Tribe.

While all these operations are in motion through the fall and winter, archaeologists are getting on with the research. Descriptive reports are written about the previous summer's field work, artifacts and photographs are catalogued, and intensive analyses of the data are undertaken. In many instances, contracts are drawn up with other individuals and institutions for specialized analysis, such as the study of the burial population or the dating of tree-ring specimens.

Long before the first dogwood blooms in southern Illinois, preparations are made for the next field season: archaeologists are hired, trucks leased, dishwashers selected, and supplies ordered.

As soon as school is out in mid-May, a caravan makes the trek to Black Mesa for the summer. When field work is completed at the end of August, BMAP recommends to the National Park Service that provisional clearance be given to Peabody to mine. The Park Service then advises clearance to the U.S. Geological Survey which grants Peabody the provisional clearance. If for any number of reasons, such as the Park Service finding our work unacceptable, clearance would not be granted, Peabody could not obtain its mining permit, and mining would grind to a halt. This places awesome responsibility on the archaeologist. Fortunately, BMAP has never been placed in this situation.

After publication of a report (usually in the spring or summer after field work) describing briefly the results of the excavations, final clearance is recommended to the Park Service by BMAP. If the report is satisfactory, the National Park Service recommends clearance to the U.S. Geological Survey which notifies Peabody that the shovels can operate.

The law, archaeology, and the coal company have been served, albeit with tremendous effort and patience, only a fraction of which involves archaeological excavation.

4
The Archaeologist in the Field And in the Lab

HOW DO ARCHAEOLOGISTS go about investigating a poorly known region? What strategies and techniques do they employ to determine what is in a particular study area, what it relates to, and roughly how old it is?

The first efforts are devoted to archaeological survey, a reconnaissance that normally does not involve excavation but determines what can be deduced about past human occupation from surface remains. Surveys have become quite sophisticated and can provide a vast array of information. Archaeologists working in the Anasazi cultural region are fortunate in that they do not have to start from scratch.

Years of survey and excavation in the area have documented that certain architectural and artifact styles indicate a general time period and cultural affiliation for the remains; as a result, BMAP's initial surveys gave us much important information about the nature of the occupation because we could fit our data into an already existing framework. Before discussing the methods and results of the Black Mesa surveys, it is advantageous to understand how archaeologists order and interpret the surface remains to make sense of questions relating to time and space.

THE PRESENT IS THE KEY TO THE PAST

All archaeologists, indeed all people, make use of what they know about human nature to draw inferences about why people behave as they do. Ethnographic analogy is a slightly more sophisticated form of this. It involves using the results of studies about living peoples to make inferences about other living or extinct groups. For example, detailed knowledge of how Australian aborigines chip a stone spear point may be used to understand how European paleolithic hand axes were manufactured.

While the value of ethnographic analogy is widely recognized in archaeological circles, archaeologists have not been able to use it as effectively as they might. This is because ethnographers, those scholars who study living groups, usually do not record the kinds of information archaeologists find useful. Ethnographers tend to be interested in such things as how husbands act toward their mothers-in-law; archaeologists are interested in, for example, why artifacts vary in shape, what the spatial relationships of artifacts used for craft and subsistence are, and how artifacts and food residue are exposed.

Because archaeologists need to interpret the residue of past human behavior, and much of the data needed for the interpretation is often not available, they have taken to doing their own ethnographic studies. Archaeologists in the last few years have been living with the Hopi to see how mothers train their daughters in pottery making, with Eskimos to understand butchering and bone disposal patterns, and with warring Philippine peoples in order to study the spatial arrangements of artifacts at habitation sites. A most famous case involves the study of garbage disposal in Tucson, Arizona, to understand the eating and drinking habits of a large, ethnically diverse, modern city.

This new activity on the part of archaeologists has been called "living" or "action" archaeology, but is most commonly known as ethnoarchaeology. By whatever name, it is an attempt to understand the archaeological record by actually observing how artifacts are made, destroyed, or discarded, to understand the processes affecting them after discard, and to understand the observer's perception of them after a period of some time.

Ethnographic analogies can then be made from the study of living people to the extinct culture under investigation. There are two kinds of ethnographic analogy. The first kind involves a situation in which two cultures have a direct connection in time and space; that is, where the living or ethnographically recorded culture has a traceable relationship to the archaeological remains. The Hopi and the Black Mesa Anasazi are an example of this type of ethnographic analogy. There is no question that the Hopi are the direct descendants of the Anasazi. The evolution of architecture and artifact styles, as well as the physical location of the Hopi, demonstrate the cultural and genetic relationship. There is even an example of a vessel found in a pithouse, dated to the ninth century, that depicts dancers wearing headdresses of a style still used today.

This kind of analogy, which permits a direct cultural connection between the two societies being compared, is invaluable for certain kinds of studies. Archaeologists interested in the evolution of Black Mesa Anasazi social organization can take the Hopi as the known end result, determine relationships between artifacts and social organization, then trace those relationships back in time. It is a process of working from the present and the known, back in time to the unknown.

The second general type of ethnographic analogy is drawn when there is no known connection between the culture producing the archaeological remains and the one which produces the ethnographic analogue. While a superficial understanding of the two types of ethnographic analogy might suggest the inadequacy of the second type, a careful examination of the second method demonstrates this is not the case.

There are predictable trends in the evolution of human behavior. Emerging civilizations tend toward a certain kind of political-religious structure; hunters and gatherers generally divide food along specific kin-related lines, and newly emerging agriculturalists usually have women tending the crops and owning the land. These are the kinds of regularities which permit anthropology and its subdisciplines of ethnology and archaeology to be sciences. It is the patterning of human behavior that can be traced on a worldwide basis using hundreds of societies as a sample.

On Black Mesa, as the reader will see, we have used both types of ethnographic analogy. The cultural connection of the Black Mesans with the modern Hopi is exploited to demonstrate the adaptation of social organization to a harsh environment. In addition, ethnoarchaeological studies of the Navajo, who have no genetic or cultural connection with the Anasazi, are used to demonstrate that many of the Anasazi settlements may not have been occupied year round.

⍟CLASSIFICATION

Change is a universal element of human society. Behavioral change is reflected in the material residue of the behavior. It is a basic premise of archaeological theory that artifacts—humanly modified things—are the direct result of human behavior and that a detailed examination of these items and their contexts permits reconstruction of the behavior. In order to examine behavioral change it is necessary to set the behavior in time, and therefore, archaeologists usually attempt to determine which elements of the material remains of a particular culture best reflect change, and use those as period markers. As it does in all sciences, classification usually contributes to the establishment of a time and space framework and provides the working basis for almost all investigation.

The archaeologist sorts and arranges objects on the basis of certain shared characteristics. The characteristics chosen depend on the kinds of questions being asked. For example, a person on the prowl in a singles bar is likely to make an initial classification of individuals on the basis of gender rather than eye color or foot size. Classification helps bring order out of chaos; it divides a mass into different units on some logical basis. Classification also permits summary description. It allows the researcher to describe a group of objects without having to describe the individual variation of each object.

Finally, classification makes it easier to see relationships between groups of objects. Similarities and differences between classes suggest degrees of relationships. It is the classification of animal and plant species that eventually led to the concept of biological evolution, because phylogenetic relationships were apparent in the ordering.

For the archaeologist, the ultimate goal of classification is the reconstruction of past human behavior; however, there are many intermediate steps. In the field and laboratory, obvious practical distinctions exist such as those between bone, stone, or pottery artifacts. After this elementary classification is done, artifacts must be separated into groups called types, to understand chronological and cultural relationships. Types are simply a group or class of artifacts which share certain characteristics reflecting patterning in behavior, making it possible to define and name or number them and recognize another example when found. Series of types are grouped into a typology or classificatory scheme.

Many typologies are constructed simply to categorize changes in the style of artifacts or architecture to devise a chronological sequence. Arrowheads, for example, are often grouped into types based on their shape. If the various types of arrowheads can be arranged in a series with dates assigned to each type, then sites which have a specific type of arrowhead can be assigned an approximate date.

While classification based on style change is often important in constructing chronological sequences, it usually does not directly address the kinds of behavioral change that archaeologists are most interested in. If typologies can be devised which are based on functional or technological differences, they are more apt to reflect behavioral or adaptive differences. A typology of skis could be devised based on their cosmetic or surface design. The typology could accurately reflect temporal changes in style; however, another typology based on other characteristics could distinguish between cross-country and downhill skis, racing and recreational skis. The first typology would provide chronological information and the other, functional and perhaps chronological data.

It is important to understand that while classification is absolutely essential for understanding relationships, it can also obscure them. If, for example, archaeologists construct a typology based on the style of painted decoration on ceramics rather than on the functions of the vessels, it may be difficult to distinguish cooking from serving or storage vessels; therefore, changes in food preparation and storage techniques may go unnoticed. Learning about human behavior, fossilized in artifacts, is the ultimate goal of archaeological classification.

Archaeologists try to construct a hierarchy of classifications starting with the individual attributes of a single artifact that represents the behavior of a single person and ending with many kinds of classifications of groups of artifacts that represent a culture.

In the Anasazi country numerous typologies of artifacts and architecture have been built into the Pecos Classification. While the usefulness of this sequence as a research device largely has been supplanted by other more detailed kinds of typologies, it allows southwestern archaeologists to make general comparisons and provides an example of how archaeological cultures are delineated.

Using changes in ceramic design and architectural style as a yardstick, archaeologists divided the Anasazi occupation in the Southwest into eight stages, Basketmaker I through III and Pueblo I through V, Pueblo V representing the modern Pueblo Indians. The change from Basketmaker to Pueblo was once thought to have been the result of an invasion of different peoples. This has since been disproved.

A description of the Basketmaker III period illustrates some of the traits used to construct an archaeological culture. Basketmaker III people lived in semisubterranean houses. They made and used undecorated pottery as well as a light gray ware painted with black geometric designs. The style of their stone tools changed from the earlier Basketmaker II stage, and the bow and arrow were introduced.

As is apparent, the representation of Anasazi culture in the Pecos Classification involves a combination of both stylistic and behavioral factors. The adoption of the bow and arrow in Basketmaker III permitted more effective food collection, and the introduction of pottery provided increased storage and food preparation capabilities. The presence or absence of design on the vessels, however, provides a stylistic time marker.

When possible, archaeologists prefer to work with a classification that represents meaningful distinctions in adaptive behavior, but when dealing with cultural stages, it is usually necessary to deal with both stylistic and behavioral classes.

ᗑCERAMICS

The study of ceramics provides an excellent example of how archaeologists infer past human behavior from material remains. For the Anasazi archaeologist, the classification of pottery, and especially broken pottery (potsherds or sherds) into various types is crucial. Potsherds have been the single most important artifact type used in establishing chronologies and for assigning cultural affinities and establishing behavioral patterns. There are a number of reasons for this overwhelming, and sometimes unfortunate, reliance on ceramic artifacts.

Ceramic vessels are very fragile, but once broken into sherds they last nearly forever. The only way to destroy sherds is to grind them into particles. Because of the fragility of whole vessels it was necessary for the Anasazi to construct new vessels continually, and the mounds of potsherds at some sites make it appear that the primary occupation of these people was the making and breaking of pots.

Wet clay is almost infinitely plastic and can be manipulated into virtually any shape. Grog or temper, a nonplastic material such as sand, is added to the clay to prevent cracking during the firing process. After firing, the surface can be coated with a thin wash of clay called slip, which may be a different color than the base clay. Designs can be painted, or the wet clay can be incised, polished, or left rough. While the clay is still moist, the original construction coils can be obliterated, semi-obliterated, or enhanced by various means. In short, clay is an excellent artistic medium which can reflect an almost unlimited degree of manipulation.

All artists and craftsmen work within the confines of tradition. Styles evolve; they do not spring spontaneously, without antecedents, from the maker's mind. As a result it is possible, using ceramics, to discern the evolution of a design style within a culture much as we can trace the evolution of body design in automobiles.

The Anasazi are justly famous for their technical and artistic proficiency with ceramics. While various regional differences allow archaeologists to distinguish archaeological subareas, over the entire tens of thousands of square miles of Anasazi country there is a remarkable consistency in design style and evolution. In other words, consistent design similarities are seen through time for all the Anasazi ceramic tradition, but enough differences exist that the archaeologist can distinguish regional ceramic variation within the Anasazi domain.

It is possible, however, to have too much of a good thing. Some archaeologists become so entranced by ceramics that they lose sight of what they are supposed to be studying—human behavior. They forget that ceramics are a tool for learning about the people who made them rather than an end in themselves.

Another danger in overreliance on ceramics is a tendency to uncritically equate ceramic similarity or difference with cultural similarity or difference. Shared design style does not necessarily mean shared culture. Numerous examples from around the world suggest that styles can cross-cut cultures—blue jeans and Coca-Cola are modern ones. Similarly, some prehistoric pottery designs may have become fads and been adopted by several societies with diverse cultures; temporal and cultural classifications based on a single type of artifact can lead an archaeologist to faulty conclusions.

With these caveats in mind we can examine how archaeologists look at Anasazi ceramics. While the number of attributes that an archaeologist could record and study is almost infinite, for the purposes of establishing a time and space framework for the Anasazi, a few characteristics are most important. In the Southwest these characteristics traditionally have reflected style and technology rather than function.

Form refers to the shape of a vessel. Paste color refers to the appearance of the interior of the vessel wall viewed in cross-section, independent of the source of clay and the technique of firing. Temper is the nonplastic material, such as sand, crushed rock, or crushed potsherds, which has been added to the clay to keep the vessel from cracking as it dries. Surface finish is the manner in which the surface of the vessel is treated. The surface can be scraped to a rough finish, highly polished, treated with a coat of fine clay called slip, left so the coils still show (called corrugated) or are semi-obliterated. The surface can be scratched or scored before firing while the clay is still wet. Paint, either plant or mineral, can be black, white, or red or a combination of the three colors (polychrome). For painted ceramics it is usually the color of the paint and the surface color of the vessel which determine the name of a particular pottery type. If, for example, the surface is white and the designs are black, the pottery type is referred to as "black-on-white." Design, which is what is painted on the vessel, is often the object of extremely complex study. With whole vessels or large sherds the layout of the design can be determined. Motifs are patterns of designs which reappear over large portions of the vessel. These motifs consist of individual elements which are the basic unit of design.

The broadest classes of ceramics, which are made up of a number of types, are called wares. Individual wares usually are equated with different Anasazi traditions. For example, Tusayan White ware and Tusayan Gray ware are equated with the Kayenta tradition. Mesa Verde White and Gray wares are associated with the Mesa Verde tradition, and Cibola White and Gray wares with the Chaco tradition.

Wares are subdivided into specific named types, which have all the attributes of the ware but with specific characteristics much more finely drawn. A ceramic ware can be likened to a genus and a type to a species, although no genetic implication is intended.

What is astounding, given the many factors which affect the attributes of a ceramic vessel, is that there is such great similarity. Perhaps 95 percent of all decorated Anasazi ceramic sherds and vessels are so uniformly patterned in their execution that they can be classified into types. It is this consistency in the evolution of Anasazi ceramics that permits the division of a ceramic tradition into numerous types.

As we shall see, the traditional ware and type distinctions are only one of a multitude of ways to examine ceramics for extracting cultural information. Many sophisticated new ways of looking at ceramics to answer specific questions have been developed by archaeologists in the last decade or so.

❧ DATING

Dating artifacts and sites is an important and often difficult task in archaeology. The basic archaeological dating device is the application of the Law of Superposition, borrowed from geology; that is, items found lower in a deposit were placed there earlier than those found on top of them. This law applies equally to the mess of papers on my desk and to a jumble of broken pots in a prehistoric garbage heap. The formation of layers in chronological and horizontal sequence is known as stratification, and the arrangement of the layers is stratigraphy. Sites occupied long enough to show evidence of change from phase to phase are called stratified.

Stratigraphy does not provide information for the assignment of specific calendrical dates. All that can be said is that artifacts in an upper layer are more recent than those in a lower layer. Stratigraphy did allow pioneer southwestern archaeologists to put architecture and artifacts in relative evolutionary order. Furthermore, the consistent vertical relationships observed in site after site permitted the relative chronological ordering of sites or artifacts found in an unstratified context. For example, if pottery design A is always higher in trash heaps than pottery design B, then when two sites are found, one containing nothing but design A and another containing nothing but design B, it can be assumed that the site with A is later than B and roughly contemporaneous with the occupation represented high in the trash heaps. This kind of relative dating is known as cross dating.

While relative dating was a crucial step in understanding southwestern prehistory, incredible refinements were made possible by the development of dendrochronology, or tree-ring dating. Dendrochronology is a chronometric or absolute dating technique which permits dating on the scale of our calendar year.

The principle of dendrochronology is known to anyone who has counted the annual rings on a stump to tell how old a tree was when it was cut. In many trees the width of these annual rings varies, reflecting climatic variations. The variations tend to run in cycles, setting a pattern of wide and narrow rings which are found in many trees in a particular environmental zone, and permitting specimen-to-specimen correlations. By taking the known cutting dates of modern trees, dendrochronologists match the ring pattern with older trees, always looking for overlap. Using this technique, they have developed a southwest tree-ring chronology which extends back to several hundred years before Christ (Fig. 4.1).

While dendrochronology is by far the most accurate chronometric dating technique in the Southwest, it is not foolproof. Use, rot, or insect infestation may have destroyed a beam's outer rings. Because they are difficult to cut, haul, and trim, beams were and still are reused in new structures, giving an inaccurate date for building construction. Most disappointing for southwestern archaeologists, however, is the fact that only certain species, such as piñon, Douglas fir, and ponderosa pine, are amenable to dating. Juniper, which was the preferred wood for house support beams because it was less susceptible to rot, can only occasionally be dated in many areas. Of the many thousands of specimens

Figure 4.1. Tree-ring width patterns taken from living trees can be correlated with other older trees. Gradually the pattern is worked back in time, using historic sites, then late prehistoric sites, and finally old archaeological samples. Tree specimens found in archaeological sites can then be matched against the pattern.

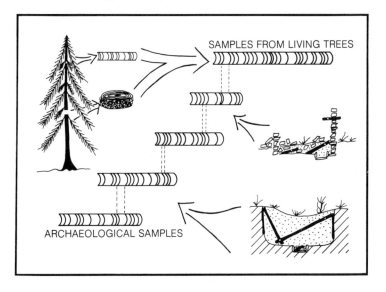

SAMPLES FROM LIVING TREES

ARCHAEOLOGICAL SAMPLES

collected by BMAP personnel, the vast majority are juniper, and only a small portion of these are datable. Given the difficulties with dendrochronology and our specific problems on Black Mesa, the thousands of hours invested in the collection, preparation, and analysis of the specimens have been worthwhile because a single date from a site, whether a cutting date or not, provides a year before which the room or structure could not have been occupied. It is a simple fact that a tree cannot be cut down and used before the year in which a ring in that tree was formed.

The combination of dendrochronology, ceramic design evolution, and the principles of cross dating has provided southwestern archaeologists with a powerful tool, dating by association. Since the development of a well-established tree-ring chronology for the Anasazi country in the 1930s, certain pottery types have been associated consistently, often in scores of different sites, with structures dated to within a certain time bracket by tree-ring evidence. Because of this it is possible to assign approximate years for the introduction of a new design style, the period of its greatest popularity, and its fall from popularity. Because a number of ceramic design styles have been dated in this manner, it is common archaeological practice to roughly date sites where potsherds litter the surface without resorting to excavation of tree-ring dating. This was possible on Black Mesa because of the well-known Kayenta ceramic design sequence and the numerous tree-ring dated sites in the region. More recently, ceramic design attributes have been correlated with tree-ring dates so that this type of dating is much more accurate.

While dendrochronology provides the most accurate dates for the Black Mesa region, when wood or ceramics are unavailable for dating by association we turn to radiocarbon dating—neither as precise nor as inexpensive as dendrochronology. The radiocarbon method measures the amount of carbon 14, a carbon isotope, remaining in organic matter. Theoretically, a living organism has a proportion of carbon 14 in it equal to that in the earth's atmosphere. When the organism dies, its carbon-14 content begins to disintegrate at a constant rate. At the end of 5,568 years, half the carbon 14 will be gone. In another 5,568 years one half of the half remaining will have disintegrated, and so on until in 50,000 to 60,000 years there is not enough carbon 14 left to measure.

Dating is accomplished by measuring the ratio of carbon 14 to other types of carbon. This does not yield a specific date, but rather a range for the age of the specimen.

A number of technical and practical problems are associated with radiocarbon analysis. Samples may be contaminated by younger organic matter (plant roots, for example) or older organic matter. Coal creates problems on Black Mesa for it is both organic and very old. A tiny fragment mixed with an archaeological sample can produce a misleading date. It is also possible that the supply of radiocarbon in the atmosphere has changed over the years so prehistoric samples may not have had the same amount of carbon 14 as organic materials have today.

Archaeomagnetic dating is another technique used to complement radiocarbon and tree-ring results, although because of the inherent limitation of the method we are only now beginning to see its use in the Southwest. Compared to other methods, archaeomagnetism as a dating tool hints at black magic. The procedure is rooted in the fact that the direction and intensity of the earth's magnetic field varies through time; when viewed from different areas of the world it shifts to the east and west by about 1° in five years.

Most clays contain magnetic particles which are not aligned in any direction. If, however, the clay is baked in a hearth, kiln, or other very hot fire, the magnetic particles align with the earth's magnetic field and the clay becomes very weakly magnetized. If the location of the geomagnetic pole in the past can be determined, the baked clay will yield a date (Fig. 4.2). The pattern of geomagnetic pole wandering for the Southwest has been established by determining the magnetic alignment of burned clay samples associated with tree-ring or radiocarbon dates. Samples without associated tree-ring or radiocarbon dates can be compared to the pattern and dated to within a 50-year period.

The pattern has to be established for relatively small areas, and on Black Mesa the paucity of cutting dates from tree-ring samples and the broad calendrical range of ceramic-derived dates has made this slow work. The long-range variation curve for Black Mesa now spans the period from A.D. 860 to 1125. This dating method will become more valuable as the curve is refined with the addition of more tree-ring and radiocarbon dates.

Figure 4.2. Clay samples from a hearth are removed after their magnetic position is recorded, permitting dating by the technique of archaeomagnetism.

There are many more potential tools for establishing a chronology than are mentioned here, but because of their expense, unreliability, or inapplicability, they have not been used on Black Mesa. When possible, tree-ring dates are preferred as the most accurate and least expensive. Dates derived from ceramic designs are also effective and inexpensive. By combining these two methods, it is possible to date sites to within a 30-year period. Radiocarbon dating is usually used for the Basketmaker II, preceramic periods.

✸ ARCHAEOLOGICAL SURVEY

The first question passersby usually ask when they see an archaeologist working at a site, especially one with few remains visible on the surface, is "How did you find it?" Usually, the answer is through systematic field survey during which all signs of artifacts or structures are recorded.

Archaeological survey is a vitally important tool for gathering information about the relationship of past people to their landscape, and as a result many questions have to be asked about the visible surface remains. There are the basic questions, such as how old is it, how big is it, what was its probable function, and so on. As archaeologists have become more sophisticated about survey, their questions have become sharper and their methods more rigorous; since most studies using survey data involve comparisons of sites, consistency in measurement and recording is essential. How BMAP survey methods and recording have changed over the years is reflected in the fact that the forms used for recording sites have grown over the years from one 5″ × 8″ card to an eight-page document.

Archaeologists now commonly cover huge areas by scientific sampling, surveying only a portion of a study area and then making statistically based inferences from what they have surveyed. Because the Black Mesa study area is being mined and the sites eventually will be destroyed, a 100 percent survey recording all visible sites has been necessary.

In theory, a site is any definable geographic space containing cultural material. In practice, many such locations must be ignored because they are nothing more than an isolated sherd or chip of stone. Recording these would greatly increase the time and cost of a survey. As a result, archaeologists sometimes have defined sites arbitrarily. For example, a site may be defined as a location that has five articles per square meter. While there are some operational problems with these examples, they are indicative of the rigor with which archaeologists are attempting to make more precise statements about surface finds.

As in most of the Southwest, sites are relatively easy to find on Black Mesa because artifacts and pit depressions are not hidden by plant cover and the color of the sherds usually contrasts with the soil.

At the beginning of BMAP, sites were located on a map and selected artifacts collected, particularly painted potsherds, since these are the best indicators of time and cultural affiliation. Sherds indicative of different time periods were especially prized because they often revealed a stratified site. Surface evidence of masonry, such as rubble mounds, upright slabs, trash deposits indicated by dark stained soil, or still-existing kiva depressions, were noted.

The early surveys in the western part of the coal lease area did not give us a great deal of hard data. Peabody Coal wanted us to survey only the locations to be mined rather than the entire lease area. This was a poor decision because each time their mining plan changed (which was often), or they had to construct a road or put in a well, it was necessary for us to return to the area to survey that section. It would have been more cost efficient and scientifically more sound to have surveyed the entire area at one time.

In 1975, Black Mesa Archaeological Project surveyed the entire lease area, not just the areas containing recognizably mineable coal, using a system of discovery, recording, and collecting that yielded much more scientifically useful information. We were notified of the need for the survey only a few weeks before the end of the summer season and the survey continued into the very cold days, and nights, of November.

The survey was done with four crews of four to six people who took about 30 days to survey one square mile. Individuals were spaced about 20 meters apart, and they walked back and forth to be sure no area was left unsearched.

Historic sites, mostly of Navajo origin, were recorded differently than prehistoric sites. If a site was historic, the location was marked on the map, a stake with the site number on it was driven into the soil and colored plastic surveyor's flagging tape was placed around the site to aid in relocating it and to alert Peabody people to its existence. Short notes were taken on the type and appearance of the site. Later, the site was revisited by an archaeologist especially interested in historical archaeology and if possible with a Navajo who knew something about the site and the people who lived in it. It was not unusual to learn that "Aunt Minnie lived there in the '40s, but had to move away when the wood supply was used up." The site was mapped, soil and ash samples were taken from hearths and storage areas, and a collection made from the trash to help in dating and determining the function of the site.

With Anasazi sites a datum, or reference point, for taking measurements was established near what appeared to be the center of the site. Then the boundaries of the site were defined by noting a relatively sharp break in the density of artifacts. Defining the site boundaries this way is quite subjective but seems to be more reasonable than the methods using an arbitrary number of artifacts per square meter. The site boundary was not determined as a continuous line, but rather at eight points starting along a line at true north from the datum and at 45° intervals from the north line. The distance along these lines to the site boundaries at eight points was then measured, providing the overall site size (Fig. 4.3).

The next step was to make a systematic collection of artifacts from within the site boundaries, making sure that enough artifacts were collected for accurate analysis and that the artifacts could be located within a 4-square-meter portion of the site. Collections were made by defining a grid system of 4 by 4 meters over the site area. If the site was smaller than 160 square meters (10 grid squares), all the artifacts from the entire site were collected, noting in which 4-square-meter unit the artifacts came from. If the site was between 160 and 1,600 square meters, 10 grid units were collected; a 10 percent sample of grid units was taken if the site was between 1,600 and 3,200 square meters; and 20 squares were collected if it was more than 3,200 square meters. This system guaranteed that for most sites we had a sufficient collection for ceramic dating purposes. It also guaranteed samples from different areas so we could determine if different parts of the site contained artifacts of varying ages suggesting occupation at different times. Also, artifacts with certain functions may be clustered in specific areas on the surface indicating that different activities were performed in those

Figure 4.3. Determination of boundaries of Anasazi site on Black Mesa. Once boundaries are drawn, artifacts are systematically collected on each site.

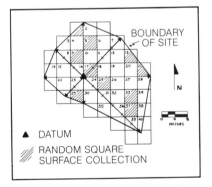

areas. The sampling technique permitted an identification of the density of the surface artifacts which might provide evidence for the function of the site or the length of its occupation. The grid units to be collected were determined randomly and were not based on artifact density. While the site was being gridded and collections made, other survey crew members recorded observations about the site on survey forms.

EXCAVATION

While archaeological survey is a very useful procedure, the ultimate weapon in the archaeologist's arsenal against the unknown is excavation. It is a weapon that has been used with increasing selectivity on Black Mesa. In the beginning, when we knew very little about the region, approximately 75 percent of the sites recorded were excavated. Later, as we became more familiar with the configuration and artifact content of various site types, we excavated only those that exhibited potential for answering questions posed in the research design.

It is seldom possible for the archaeologist to excavate a site completely except for the very smallest ones. At some point during excavation the decision has to be made to stop because the information return does not justify the time and money spent. As a result, archaeologists sample sites to varying degrees of completeness. The sampling ranges from drilling with an auger to obtain soil samples and to determine the depth and extent of the site, to excavating most of the site.

Figure 4.4. Structures such as these two round, deep pithouses are often excavated by first cutting two trenches at right angles before fill is removed. This technique permits archaeologists to study how the structure was filled before it was abandoned.

What site gets excavated and how it is done is largely determined by the archaeologist's research questions, the focal point of the research. The research

Figure 4.5. Site excavation requires both careful control, as represented by stakes in ground, and the removal of large amounts of dirt, a different goal.

questions are part of an overall research design which not only explicitly states the research questions which will be addressed, but also sets out in some detail the plan of survey, excavation, and analysis which will be used to address the research questions.

A standard set of excavation guidelines has been developed over the years on Black Mesa. For the excavation of each site a 2-by-2-meter-square grid system is established over the entire site and all surface artifacts are collected, keeping artifacts separate by each grid square. While the collection is being made, a contour map of the immediate area is drawn. The grid system and contour map form the basic horizontal control for the site which allows all artifacts and structures to be located precisely. All grids in which there are surface indications of structures or where structures are suspected are excavated, as well as an area 2 to 6 meters around the structures. If structures or other features are encountered that are partially inside the excavation square, they are also excavated. Areas outside structures or suspected structures are sampled in ways statistically determined to ensure that a good geographical spread is obtained. Sites without surface indications of structures are systematically sampled or areas with the greatest numbers of artifacts are chosen for complete excavation. Sample grids are frequently selected for excavation on the basis of artifact density, degree of ground slope, or proximity to known structures. These methods for the selection of excavation grids prevent us from systematically ignoring certain surface conditions for testing, and assure excavation of other areas deemed important for study.

While 2-by-2-meter-square grids are the basic excavation units plotted over the surface of the site on actual excavation, each sample square is divided into four 1-by-1-meter-square units to more accurately locate the horizontal position of artifacts and features, such as hearths and pits. All artifacts, seeds and bones are collected and kept separate according to soil layers which are distinguished by color or texture. If the layer is homogeneous and thicker than 20 centimeters, however, collections are made and kept separate by arbitrary 20-centimeter levels in spite of the fact that no naturally distinctive layers can be observed (Figs. 4.4 and 4.5).

In almost all instances, the dirt is screened through a one-quarter-inch mesh. When large or deep pit houses or kivas with a great

Figure 4.6. A Navajo worker fills out a computer code form, a record of where an artifact was found.

volume of dirt are encountered, a 2-by-2-meter-square pit was dug to the floor and the dirt screened. If few artifacts are found in that initial test, the rest of the fill is excavated with a trenching backhoe. The dirt near the floor of the structure is shoveled out and screened.

Modern archaeological excavation produces more paper forms, notes, and photographs than it does artifacts. Many pages of notes are taken on observations about the excavation strategy employed, artifacts, architecture, the natural environment, and so on. Because certain kinds of observations are usually made at every site, however, most archaeologists desire forms for consistency in recording. The use of forms rather than written descriptions helps ensure that necessary information is recorded since the categories on the printed form must be filled in (Fig. 4.6).

On Black Mesa, excavation forms are used for recording dirt samples taken to obtain plant and bone samples, clay and mineral samples, architectural features, provenience (or locational record of artifacts), information about postholes, records for each bag of

Figure 4.7. Vessels placed with a burial have been cleaned and are ready for analysis in the field laboratory.

material taken from field, petroglyphs or rock art panels, human burials, isolated human bones, and what we call features (isolated pits or hearths). In addition, it is not unusual to have 75 or 100 maps and sketches drawn for an average site. The paperwork would make a federal employee blush!

During and after the excavation procedure, the cleaning, description, and preliminary analysis of artifacts and other materials takes place in the laboratory in the Black Mesa camp (Fig. 4.7).

5

Seventeen Hundred & Fifty Years in the Life of Black Mesa

YEARS OF SURVEY, excavation, and analysis have enabled us to chronicle in considerable detail the evolution of Black Mesa culture history—what happened where and when. A much more difficult task, and one that is still ongoing, is explaining why Black Mesa culture evolved the way it did.

Before examining the cultural sequence of the Black Mesa Anasazi, it is important to appreciate their natural surroundings, for it was struggle with the environment that ruled their lives and shaped their history.

ANASAZI COUNTRY

Anasazi country is approximately coterminous with the southern Colorado Plateau, an area extending north from the Colorado and Little Colorado rivers in Arizona into southeast Utah, the southwest corner of Colorado, and the northwest corner of New Mexico. While there is considerable environmental diversity on the Colorado Plateau, the area shares a number of features.

Elevation is relatively high, ranging from about 4,000 to 12,000 feet. The topography is rugged, dominated by plateaus and mesas with narrow canyons and wide valleys separating them, and marked by such extreme geological manifestations as the Grand Canyon and the towering San Francisco Peaks north of Flagstaff.

Rainfall, the lifeblood of both prehistoric and modern farmers, is quite erratic, averaging about 11 inches annually, increasing from 8 inches in the lower elevations to 13 or so at the higher ones. While rainfall is equally divided between summer and winter seasons, the winter precipitation, often in the form of snow, tends to occur over a longer period of time. Summer thundershower activity is short and intense. Summer storms usually start around mid-July and continue into September. Thunderheads build to tremendous heights, then burst, inundating local areas. Washes become raging rivers, gullies form, and the earth's surface is turned into a quagmire. Floods often destroy bridges, buildings, or anything else in their way. Moisture usually does not penetrate the soil very deeply and rapid runoff is normal. Soon after the end of the thunderstorm the soil is dry, and the most notable effects are a fresh smell in the air, a greening of the vegetation from having been washed clean, and a deepening of erosional channels.

Most of the Colorado Plateau is dominated by piñon and juniper woodlands and sagebrush flats. The piñon-juniper areas tend to cluster between 5,000 and 6,500 feet with juniper dominant in the lower part of the range and piñon in the higher. Sagebrush, Indian rice grass, black grama, blue grama, and galleta grass also favor the lower elevations down to about 4,000 feet, especially the alluvium-filled valleys and basins. Because of overgrazing and climate change in historic times, snakeweed has invaded much of the land and large, eroded sections are sometimes completely denuded, leaving huge stretches of badlands.

Also because of overgrazing and overhunting, native animals are relatively scarce. Mule deer, bear, elk, mountain lion, and wild turkey are found at higher elevations, and antelope and jackrabbit in the mid to lower elevations. The unbelievably adaptable coyote is ubiquitous.

It is a common misconception that in prehistoric times the grass was waist-high and the countryside overrun with game. While erosion was not as bad then as it is now, all indications are that the climate was not too different from today. Plant and animal species differed somewhat in frequency of occurrence, but by and large what we see is what the Anasazi saw.

Black Mesa is one of the most prominent geographic features in the Southwest. Its maximum elevation in the northeast is some 8,000 feet, although the average elevation along the northern escarpment is about 6,800 to 7,000 feet. The elevation drops considerably to the south and toward the interior of the mesa. The terrain is fairly consistent in appearance, with undulating hills dissected by intricate systems of small, deeply cut washes draining into Moenkopi Wash and other large drainages. These washes cut through the southern part of the mesa, forming the "fringes" on which the Hopi towns are found. Black Mesa is so large and the topography so rolling and consistent that one has no feeling of being on an elevated land mass. Only when you are near the edge of the escarpment does the elevation become apparent.

While there is, and probably was, no permanent stream on Black Mesa, water usually can be found by digging a few feet into the sandy bottom of a major wash. A few scattered seeps and springs are also present.

Vegetation varies little over the entire mesa. Piñon and juniper with sage flats and some grasslands dominate the landscape. The vegetation is highly reflective of elevation. Douglas-fir, aspen, ponderosa pine, and Gambel oak are found in moist isolated pockets at the highest elevations. The grasslands become more expansive in the lower elevations of the southern part of the mesa.

Climate is typical of the Colorado Plateau at these elevations— cold winters with snow, warm summers with temperatures as high as 100°F.

THE CULTURAL SEQUENCE

For areas of the Southwest where a great deal of archaeological survey and excavation have been done, general cultural sequences can be divided into finer temporal units for relatively small geographic zones. The geographically bounded, relatively short segments of cultural history are called phases. The temporal sequence of phases for a specific area is called a regional sequence. The Black Mesa regional sequence is more detailed, more precisely dated, and geographically limited than the broad Pecos Classification (see Table 5.1).

The culture of the Black Mesa people was part of the Anasazi tradition known as the Kayenta variant. At their maximum extent the Kayenta people occupied an area of more than 10,000 square miles, and while variation is apparent in the archaeology within this large area, it is possible to make generalizations.*

People first entered the Four Corners region thousands of years before Christ, although only traces of their past activities remain. They were a seminomadic people who subsisted by hunting and gathering wild plant foods, a pattern common over much of the arid West at that time. These Archaic people left few material remains. Seed-crushing implements (mortar- and pestle-like grinding tools), spear points, small stone hide- and woodworking tools are the most common artifacts from this period.

Several prehistoric cultures have been identified within this Archaic stage. In the Kayenta region, the best known is the very

Table 5.1 **The Pecos Classification and the Black Mesa Regional Sequence**

Pecos Classification	Black Mesa Phases
Basketmaker II	Lolomai (600 B.C.–A.D. 400)
Basketmaker III	Dot Klish (A.D. 600–750)
Basketmaker III–Pueblo I	Tallahogan (A.D. 750–850)
Pueblo I	Dinnebito (A.D. 850–975)
Pueblo I–II	Wepo (A.D. 975–1050)
Early Pueblo II	Lamoki (A.D. 1050–1100)
Late Pueblo II	Toreva (A.D. 1100–1150)
Early Pueblo III	Klethla (A.D. 1150–1250)
Late Pueblo III	Tsegi (A.D. 1250–1300)

---

* In the following culture-history discussion, Black Mesa phase names refer to specific Black Mesa manifestations. When generalizing to the Anasazi as a whole, the Pecos Classification will be used.

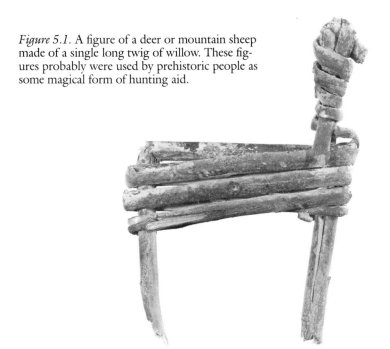

Figure 5.1. A figure of a deer or mountain sheep made of a single long twig of willow. These figures probably were used by prehistoric people as some magical form of hunting aid.

early Desha Complex which dates to between 5000 and 6000 B.C. Desha Complex remains—food-grinding tools, sandals, and a few small knives and projectile points—have been excavated in the Navajo Mountain area. The artifacts indicated the economy was oriented more to the collecting of wild plant foods than to hunting. Large, Ice Age animals had long since become extinct.

A few arrowheads, scrapers, and other stone artifacts dating to about 2000 B.C. are occasionally found in northern Arizona and Utah. These are grouped under the title Pinto Complex. Perhaps associated with the Pinto Complex are the fascinating split-willow twig animal figurines, only a few inches long, found in caves in the Grand Canyon and its vicinity. These figures, which resemble mountain sheep or deer, are sometimes pierced with what appears to be a spear, and are always found far from habitation areas (Fig. 5.1). This suggests that they were used to help ensure hunting success. They may well be the southwestern equivalent of early European cave paintings.

Lolomai Phase (Basketmaker II), 600 B.C. to A.D. 400

The earliest human occupation of Black Mesa for which we have evidence occurred during the Lolomai phase. Undoubtedly some earlier, Archaic people, perhaps the makers of the split-twig figurines or people of the Desha Complex, traversed the area following game or collecting seeds and piñon nuts. If they established campsites on the mesa, the sites have not been located.

Basketmaker II remains dating to about A.D. 400 are found on Black Mesa and throughout Anasazi country. While Basketmaker II sites on Black Mesa yield radiocarbon samples several centuries older than samples from other areas, no claim is made for the primacy of the period on Black Mesa. Few Basketmaker II sites anywhere have been radiocarbon dated, and few have been excavated using modern techniques.

The Basketmaker II stage is important because it represents the beginnings of agriculture in the Kayenta area and, therefore, the ability of the nomadic people to establish large, relatively permanent villages. This shift did not occur overnight. At first, the low-yield crops of corn and squash only supplemented wild plant foods. Dependence on them increased gradually.

The addition of corn and squash to the Anasazi diet was not the result of independent invention. The plants and cultivating techniques came from Mexico via the Mogollon peoples of the mountain regions of central Arizona. Although the mechanism by which the domesticated plants found their way north is unknown, their spread probably was due to a gradual extension of the environmental zone in which they could be grown rather than to long-range trading.

Evidence for Lolomai occupation of Black Mesa was first discovered during the summer of 1973. Since then, numerous Lolomai sites have been recorded and excavated. These sites probably were not discovered earlier because they are so difficult to see; the only surface clue to their presence is a scattering of nondescript chipped white siltstone. Few finished artifacts are found on the surface, and pottery was not yet part of Anasazi material culture (Figs. 5.2 and 5.3).

While material remains of Lolomai sites are relatively scant, remains of Basketmaker II people have been excavated in caves north and east of Black Mesa. Some of the richest of these dry,

Figure 5.2. A typically nondescript Lolomai phase site. Storage pits are usually scattered around the site. All that remains of most houses are shallow depressions with post and storage holes in the floor.

artifact-crammed caves are in the Kayenta culture area. The most famous is White Dog Cave, some 12 miles east of the town of Kayenta, within sight of Black Mesa.

Since there is considerable correspondence between the non-perishable remains left by Lolomai phase people on Black Mesa and those of the Basketmaker II people recovered to the north and east, it is possible to make analogies between the two. We know, for example, how these people dressed, how they made their baskets, and, because flesh and hair are often preserved in the caves, what their facial features and hairstyles were like.

Figure 5.3. Crude masonry walls occasionally shape the edge of Lolomai pit-houses.

The initial occupation of Black Mesa was sparse, for although we have now recorded a relatively large number of Lolomai sites, the phase is so long, some 800 years, that few of the communities were contemporaneous. Often when population was low on Black Mesa, settlements tended to be close to springs and washes to take advantage of available water. This was not the case during the Lolomai phase; villages were situated on ridges at higher elevations, perhaps to provide a good view of game, other communities, or even the spectacular southwestern sunsets.

Sites are often found near open sagebrush flats with their deep fertile alluvium. Corn has been recovered from most Lolomai sites, and squash is found in Basketmaker II sites off the mesa.

Hunting was done both with nets and snares as well as with atlatls. An atlatl is a throwing stick which has the effect of lengthening the arm, permitting the user to hurl a spear with increased force and accuracy. A wide variety of ingenious snares made of human hair were used to catch small game. Large plant-fiber nets resembling tennis nets were used to block off canyons so that small animals, mostly rabbits, could be driven into them and killed. One net recovered in White Dog Cave contained almost four miles of string and weighed twenty-eight pounds. Dogs were probably used in hunting also.

The Basketmaker economy involved agriculture, hunting animals, and collecting wild plants, but the ratio of one to the other is not known. Too few sites have been excavated to permit site-to-site and period-to-period comparisons. It is known that the type of corn and its yield in Lolomai sites is similar to that in later sites. Probably, however, meat and wild nuts and seeds provided the major components of the diet, since corn was newly introduced.

Wild and domesticated plant material was prepared by grinding in a basin metate with a one-hand mano, although the more efficient two-hand mano and trough metate were beginning to evolve. Since ceramic vessels were not yet available, cooking was done directly over an open fire or in baskets. Woven, watertight baskets were filled with food and water, and hot stones were dropped in.

Lolomai sites consist of dwelling and storage pits, none of which would be featured in *House Beautiful*. Usually the houses are simple saucer-shaped depressions in the ground with a brush and mud upper wall (Figs. 5.4 and 5.5). Occasionally the houses are excavated deeper, even into bedrock. The floor is never well prepared and is often very uneven. Storge pits are constructed in the same manner but are occasionally slab lined. Often the only difference between a storage pit and a dwelling is the presence of a hearth in the dwelling.

Lolomai sites do not exhibit any particular patterning, either

Figure 5.4. A Lolomai dwelling partially excavated into the soil. The upper parts of the walls were constructed of poles and mud that has long since disintegrated.

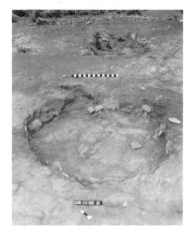

architecturally or regarding location of features within a site. Communities were small, probably consisting of a few related families. Many of the sites are so small that they may well have been occupied only seasonally. Because Lolomai sites are not really numerous on Black Mesa and because they span an 800-year period, it is impossible to determine what kinds of social and economic relationships may have existed between communities. No two sites may even have been contemporaneous!* Basketmaker II sites off the mesa, however, can be very large, indicating a different kind of community organization.

As in later periods, some interaction between Lolomai and other Basketmaker II communities must have occurred for there are shared stylistic patterns in architecture and artifacts. Basketmaker II sites often contain olivella and abalone shell beads which were traded in from the Pacific coast. It is sobering to realize that these isolated, simple agriculturalists had access to such a far-reaching trade network.

Dot Klish Phase (Basketmaker III), A.D. 600 to 750

The Basketmaker III stage was a period of many innovations, such as the introduction of the bow and arrow, domesticated beans, and pottery. Population increased and pithouse architecture became more substantial and formalized. Surface masonry or jacal storage structures were common. Villages were often very large and occasionally included large structures known as kivas. The increased size and permanence of the occupations, which seems to have depended on favorable environmental locations, indicate an increased reliance on cultivated crops.

At some sites, especially large kivas, called great kivas, are found. Great kivas are more common in later Anasazi periods and are presumed to indicate a degree of religious and economic cooperation between villages because they often appear to have been too large to serve the needs of a single community. The existence of

---

*On the other hand, radiocarbon dates indicate that many of the sites were occupied just before the time of Christ. This suggests that contemporaneous groups of people inhabited the mesa for a century.

one great kiva at the site of Juniper Cove in the Kayenta district at the base of Black Mesa suggests social, religious, and economic interaction between villages for at least some of the Basketmaker III communities on the mesa.

While thousands of Basketmaker III sites have been recorded and more than a hundred excavated in the Anasazi country, this period is very poorly represented on northeastern Black Mesa. Excavations along the coal slurry pipeline from Black Mesa westward to Nevada and along a road on the central and southern section of the mesa provide some evidence for understanding this period.

Several explanations can be offered for the scarcity of Dot Klish phase sites in the coal lease area. Possibly, most of the sites were located along flood plains of the major washes and have since been buried by silting. Early sites are often seen in the exposed face of arroyo cuts as much as 2 meters below the present ground surface. Most of the Dot Klish phase sites were discovered when they were uncovered by construction activity.

It seems unreasonable, however, that *all* Dot Klish phase sites would be buried. Thus the explanation is probably that population on northern Black Mesa was quite low at this time. Since Dot Klish phase sites are found south and southwest of the coal lease areas in somewhat better-watered regions with a longer growing season, the environment may be the reason for the extremely low population. Basketmaker III sites are usually located along broad alluvium-filled valleys which have high water tables, or in dense sand dune areas. Barren sand dunes, for all their dry and desolate look, actually conserve moisture and make excellent gardening locations. The Hopis at the southern end of Black Mesa plant crops in sand dunes today.

Figure 5.5. A Lolomai storage pit excavated in bedrock

With a low population and increasing dependence on agriculture, the concentration of population in these more agriculturally favorable locations makes good sense. Sand dunes are not found in the coal mine lease areas and choice alluvium-filled valleys are located farther south and west. There was no need to use the less desirable areas for habitation when the small population allowed construction of villages close to prime agricultural land.

Whatever the reason, it is unfortunate that Basketmaker III is so poorly represented on northern Black Mesa, for it was a period of great change in Anasazi culture.

The introduction of ceramics, beans, the bow and arrow, more formalized architecture, occasional large specialized ceremonial rooms, and an increase in population all indicate increased reliance on agriculture, a more settled existence, a more energy efficient economy, and complex inter- and intracommunity relations.

The Anasazi diet was improved considerably by the addition of protein-rich beans to the corn and squash already being eaten. Because corn varieties vary tremendously in productivity, it is important to know the variety of corn to determine the potential importance of that crop in the diet. Enough corn was recovered from Dot Klish phase sites along the pipeline on western Black Mesa to provide an accurate picture of its role in the diet. The corn is small to medium in size but relatively productive. A strain similar to it is still grown by the Hopi. It is also similar to corn found in other Basketmaker III sites off the mesa. However, a larger proportion of somewhat older, smaller sizes suggests that greater conservatism on Black Mesa may have kept the older strains in popularity. In any case, the corn was productive enough that it could have been a mainstay of the diet. Protein in the form of animal meat was also easier to obtain with the newly introduced bow and arrow, a more accurate and effective long distance hunting tool than the spear and atlatl.

While diet had been improved and the subsistence base made more secure, the Dot Klish people may have been severely hampered by disease. Human feces found on the floor of a pithouse excavated along the slurry line on western Black Mesa showed that the individual was suffering from a massive infestation of parasitic spiny-headed worms (*Acanthocephalans*). According to the biologist who examined the feces, the infection was sufficiently severe that the person may have died from internal bleeding. Because spiny-headed worms are extremely infectious, their presence may have caused severe problems for these people and, in fact, may partially explain the low Dot Klish phase population. Feces recovered from later phase sites do not contain the parasites, but this may be an accident of differential discovery.

Like the domesticated crops, ceramics probably originated in Mexico. Along with more permanent structures, larger villages, and an increased reliance on domesticates, they suggest that life was more settled and less nomadic. Ceramic vessels are efficient cooking and storage containers, but are short lived when used by nomadic or seminomadic people. While the pottery is not as artistically and technically sophisticated as later Kayenta pottery, it does not represent the earliest dabbling in clay. Bowls are often coated with a white background on which grey geometric designs are painted. Plain grey bowls and jars with a rough sandy surface are also made. Even the increasing use of the more efficient two-hand mano and metate suggests a greater reliance on agriculture and the need to process grain more efficiently.

Dot Klish phase sites provide evidence for modest use of coal, more than a thousand years before the arrival of Peabody Coal Company on Black Mesa. There are large, late-prehistoric coal mines on the southern edge of Black Mesa where coal seams are exposed at the edge of the mesa along the face of the cliffs. These were worked in Pueblo IV times by digging back into the cliffs with picks made of deer antlers. The coal was then used for heating and for firing pottery. For all earlier periods on Black Mesa, however, the use of coal for fuel was minimal. Coal ash in the hearth of a Dot Klish phase pithouse proves that coal was used occasionally for fuel, although the noxious fumes must have made the interior of the dwelling anything but pleasant. While a coal fire lasts longer than one of wood, the abundance of piñon and juniper in the area should have made it the preferred fuel for cooking and home heating.

There are real advantages in using coal to fire ceramics, however. A coal fire is hotter, takes longer to build to a peak temperature, and keeps a higher temperature longer than a wood fire, all desirable characteristics in pottery making. A very low percentage of potsherds indicates firing at a higher temperature. They are distinguished by a yellow cast to the normally white background, and the decoration is a rust or orange yellow rather than black. Sometimes the design is visible only as a "ghost" pattern, the paint having been burned off. Furthermore, these sherds have a high degree of clay vitrification. They are almost glasslike and their fracture is sharp and hard rather than crumbly. Jeff King, then an undergraduate at Prescott College, tried to determine if coal was used for the firing of these vessels with a yellowish cast. He refired ordinary black-on-white sherds in a modern kiln above the normal firing temperature of wood fires at 675° to 850° C. At about 900° C. the refired pottery took on the characteristics of the sherds assumed to have been coal fired. Since that temperature is well within the range of a coal-fueled fire and there is evidence that coal was used in dwelling firepits, presumably coal was used occasionally to fire ceramics.

The potters, however, did not apparently perceive the benefits of firing their wares at a higher temperature until the Pueblo IV period, because from the introduction of ceramics in the Dot Klish phase until the abandonment of northern Black Mesa, the percentage of coal-fired ceramics remained at about 0.1. The pre-Pueblo IV coal-fired pottery may have been an accidental and undesirable product to be recreated only occasionally.

The only Black Mesa artifacts made of coal are found at Wepo phase sites. They are small, polished coal buttons or pendants with holes drilled through them, presumably so they could be suspended from a string and used as a piece of jewelry.

Basketmaker III communities usually were much larger than earlier ones. While some communities had only four or five houses, others had up to twenty. The increased size indicates a community-wide social organization that involved more than one or two extended families.

Individual dwellings are small, round, deep pithouses with wood and mud superstructures. The houses have a fire pit and often a dividing ridge of clay or slabs extending from the fire pit to the house walls, partitioning the floor. The purpose of this partition is a mystery. Opposite the fire pit is an opening in the wall which extends to the surface and provides ventilation. A slab, called a deflector, is placed between the fire pit and the ventilation opening to deflect the incoming air away from the fire, moving the draft upward and out of the entry hole in the roof, taking the smoke from the fire with it. Sometimes an arch of slab-lined storage structures curves around one side of a line of pithouses.

Most of these architectural traits are found at Dot Klish phase villages in the central and western portions of Black Mesa, out of the immediate coal lease area, although the communities are smaller and the configuration less formal than in many other Anasazi areas. Many of these larger villages represent a considerable investment in energy and probably are not the result of temporary or seasonal encampments.

While Dot Klish phase people were simple farmers living in dispersed small communities, evidence has been found of considerable contact between communities within the Kayenta country and even with the Mogollon communities to the south. The great kivas found at Basketmaker III sites indicate intercommunity contact on a religious level. Seldom, however, do such large ceremonial structures serve a single function. If the great kivas were part of a pan-village religious organization, they probably also served as places for trade in tools, food, and ideas; for meeting and engaging prospective spouses; and for the discussion of common problems.

These early great kivas are sufficiently rare that it can be said that they were not an essential element in the bonding of Anasazi communities. In fact, the Juniper Cove great kiva is the only one found for any phase in the Kayenta area. For whatever reason, the Kayenta Anasazi did not have or need the great kivas employed by other Anasazi groups.

The close and continual relationships that did exist between communities throughout the Kayenta country beginning in the Dot Klish phase are demonstrated by the great similarity of ceramic vessel form and painted design. The only other explanation for the parallel evolution of ceramic crafts over such a large area is that only one or two centers of ceramic production existed. This is unlikely given the seeming provincialism of Dot Klish communities.

Beyond a handful of shell, few exotic items from some distance outside the region were traded onto Black Mesa. At a village along the slurry pipeline, however, a single Forestdale Smudged bowl made in the Mogollon country far to the south was found in a storage pit. The vessel is brown, intentionally darkened in a smoky fire, and was made not by placing coil on top of coil, but rather by forming a single large lump of clay into a container. This is a ceramic tradition of the Mogollon rather than the Anasazi. What was traded in the bowl or why the bowl itself was traded is unknown, but it does indicate contact between the two areas.

The Basketmaker III period–Dot Klish phase was a time of intense cultural innovation and experimentation which paved the way for the large Anasazi communities practicing intensive agriculture, culminating in the large Pueblo towns the Spanish encountered many centuries later.

Tallahogan Phase (Basketmaker III–Pueblo I), A.D. 750 to 850

There is little to say about the Tallahogan phase, since as with the Dot Klish phase few sites of this period were found in the lease area. One buried pithouse was found along a wash when a trenching machine excavating for a pipeline cut through the structure. The pithouse was buried so deeply that it was not possible to determine if there were other structures at the site. Several other Tallahogan communities were recorded near the pipeline; however, they are outside the right of way and could not be excavated. Enough surface indications are visible so that some generalizations can be made.

Communities were still situated near sand dunes and along major washes during this phase to take advantage of the better agricultural environments. Rather than being located on the lowest terrace directly above the stream bed as is often the case with Dot Klish villages, they tend to be situated on a higher terrace. This slight locational shift may have been due to the need to use the former habitation zone for agriculture because of a slightly larger population.

The Tallahogan economy differed little from the economy of the preceding Dot Klish phase. There are not enough tool types to be able to infer any possible shift in the subsistence base, and no food remains other than animal bones were found.

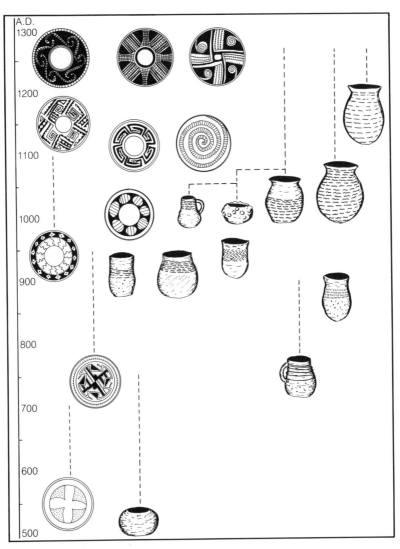

Figure 5.6. The evolution of black-on-white and unpainted ceramics. Ceramic analysis can help immensely in dating archaeological sites.

Ceramics became more sophisticated during the Tallahogan phase. While the rough-surfaced type called Lino Black-on-gray and Lino Gray of the earlier period were still produced, or at least used, the highly polished Kana-a Black-on-white was more in vogue (Fig. 5.6).

Villages were more formally laid out, at least those villages that were inhabited year round. Pithouses were arranged in a rough line, and in back of them was an area of contiguous slab-lined semi-subterranean storage pits. This is a pattern often found at village sites dating to this period throughout Anasazi country. The sites along the pipeline have the upright slabs poking up above the sand, forming an arc. There are slight depressions in front of them, usually an indication of deep subsurface structures.

The buried pithouse that was cut by the pipeline was well constructed and seemed to be for year-round occupation. The structure had burned with such intensity that the surrounding sand and clay was brick hardened as much as 9 inches behind the walls. The fire hardened and preserved much of the architectural detail. The circular structure was sunk about 3 feet into the sand. Upright juniper poles were plastered into the wall about a foot apart to stabilize it in the sandy soil. The upper part of the walls and roof were made of beams and brush plastered over with mud in a technique known as jacal (Fig. 5.7). A low ridge of clay from the fire pit to the walls divided the floor of the pithouse. Abutting the fire pit was a slab-lined hole in the floor which was a receptacle for the overflow of ash from the fire pit. Instead of a deflector slab, the ventilator shaft opened in two different places so that the incoming draft was routed away from the hearth. Two slabs which fit over the ventilator shaft openings were leaning against the walls near the openings and were used to block the air flow during inclement weather. The double ventilator shaft opening seems to have been a common feature during this period.

Dinnebito Phase (Pueblo I), A.D. 850 to 975

Basketmaker III evolved into Pueblo I without major or abrupt behavioral changes as might be suggested by the stage designations. Archaeologists originally believed the Pueblo I period was

Figure 5.7. Part of a damaged room in a cliff dwelling exposing a section of jacal wall. Sticks and reeds are covered with mud to form a sturdy structure.

marked by the migration of a new people into the area because of the sudden presence of individuals with a pronounced flattening of the back of the skull. Later this was discovered to have been the result of strapping infants in cradle boards which deformed the young malleable skull.

Pueblo I communities usually consisted of several pithouses with groups of contiguous, surface, slab-walled masonry or jacal storage units. No great kivas dating to this time have been found

Figure 5.8. Dinnebito phase sites are often located in sagebrush-covered areas in the uplands, like this site under excavation.

in the Kayenta region, suggesting that villages may have been more autonomous.

In most Anasazi regions a black-on-red ceramic tradition was introduced, although what this means in terms of invention or contact with other groups is not known.

The Dinnebito phase was a period of major change for the people of Black Mesa. During this phase a definite increase in population occurred, a trend which continued in later phases. There are more Dinnebito phase sites, and they are larger, containing from four to eighteen structures. Furthermore, each dwelling is somewhat bigger than in previous phases, confirming the fact that family size was increasing.

Toward the end of the Dinnebito phase, upland areas away from the larger drainages were used more frequently for village sites. These communities usually were located at the edge of sagebrush flats or basins that had deep soil where moisture collected (Fig. 5.8).

This shift in the pattern of settlement probably was caused by two factors. As population increased, the more favorable environmental niches along the washes were filled or were used for farming instead of habitation. At the same time the climate became slightly wetter and cooler, permitting farming of the uplands. This situation will be discussed at greater length in a later section.

Maize seemed to be an economic mainstay. The percentage of that crop recovered in relationship to other plant foods is quite high for this time period. The vast majority of the manos from this period are of the two-hand variety, a more efficient grinding tool.

Decorated ceramics were dominated by the polished, well-fired, and beautifully executed Kana-a Black-on-white. An undecorated, rough gray type of vessel, called Kana-a Gray, was also used.

A shift from subsurface to surface dwellings and the use of true layered masonry began during this phase. The transition was not rapid nor was there a complete switch in orientation. Most villages retained a mix of underground and surface dwellings. Also during the Dinnebito phase some subsurface structures took on the more formal characteristics of kivas. While archaeologists call these structures kivas, they may not have had precisely the same function that modern kivas do for the Pueblo Indians. Nevertheless, shared characteristics make it obvious that the kiva of Dinnebito times evolved into the modern Pueblo kiva.

A good example of a Dinnebito phase site is Az. D:7:134, one of a cluster of three such sites located a sherd's throw from one another. A close examination of this site provides not only an accurate perspective on a Dinnebito phase community, but also some insights into archaeological method.

The village is in the configuration of later Anasazi communities with a line of contiguous masonry surface rooms fronted by a deep pit structure, probably a kiva. The major trash heap is on the opposite side of the kiva. Various shallow pithouses and jacal and masonry rooms are scattered, seemingly at random, between the line of masonry rooms and the kiva.

Architectural detail varies greatly at Az. D:7:134, as might be expected for a period when structural style was rapidly changing. Especially great variation is seen in the style of masonry. Most of the masonry rooms are only partially above the surface. Slabs are sometimes placed upright some 50 centimeters below the surface, and roughly shaped sandstone blocks fitted with a great deal of mud mortar are placed on the upright slabs. While masonry on

Black Mesa was never very elegant, Dinnebito style masonry often seems to be the result of haphazardly piling rocks on top of one another and filling the cracks with mud. The walls were quite unstable and probably did not stand too long after abandonment.

Most of the pithouses were rectangular with rounded corners and only a foot or two deep. The upper part of the walls was of pole-and-mud construction as was the roof. While called a pithouse, most of the house was above ground.

Not all the structures at the village were in use at the same time, making it difficult for archaeologists to determine population figures based on the number of rooms occupied at any one time. Current population figures for New York City would be similarly biased if all the burned, vandalized, and abandoned apartments in the South Bronx were considered to be occupied.

Sometimes it is easy to tell earlier structures from later ones because earlier rooms are filled with later period trash or a later house is superimposed over an earlier structure. Most attempts at establishing contemporaneity or a building sequence are not so easy. If a block of rooms exists, it is possible to determine if it was constructed as a single unit or if rooms were added, simply by looking at how the interior walls meet the exterior walls. If, for example, the exterior walls are constructed along the entire length of the roomblock and the interior walls abut the exterior walls, it is safe to assume that the roomblock was planned and built as a single unit. On the other hand, if exterior walls abut other exterior walls, the abutting walls had to be constructed later than the wall to which they are abutted. The time between construction periods may be ten minutes or ten years (Fig. 5.9).

At Az. D:7:134 most exterior masonry walls abut other exterior walls. Superimposed and trash-filled structures also indicate that the village was not constructed as a single unit and was not abandoned at one time.

An ingenious method for refining the structure occupation sequence was developed by Anthony Klesert, then an SIU graduate student. He used degrees of similarity in ceramic design elements to date structures relatively. The basic assumption of Klesert's test is that design elements change slightly over generations and that by measuring their degree of similarity, rooms or clusters of rooms can be grouped as being most similar and by inference most closely associated in time. His results could be partially tested at the site

Figure 5.9. Wall construction can give a clue to building sequence. The cross wall of this room abuts and is not bonded to the other walls, indicating that it was constructed later in the sequence.

by tree-ring dates, by wall abutting patterns, and by the stratigraphy of structures superimposed over other structures. Using these techniques, he determined that rooms 4, 5, and 6 and jacal rooms 17 and 18 seem to be the latest at the site and that pithouses 11 and 14 are the earliest (Fig. 5.10). Pithouses 12 and 13 appear to be relatively late and contemporaneous with masonry rooms 8 and 9. Pithouse 2 is associated with rooms 7, 8, 9 and 10 and so on. The interesting thing is that almost all the decorated black-on-white sherds were classified only as the type called Kana-a, and therefore an attempt to date the relationship of one structure to another using traditional ceramic types would have failed because standard ceramic types are not discriminating enough.

Susan Chandler, a student from the University of Colorado, attempted to define the social organization for Dinnebito phase sites and the social relationships of the three sites in close proximity to one another.

For various anthropological reasons she believed that the Dinnebito communities were made up of lineages and more specifically, matrilineages. A lineage is a group of descendants of a known common ancestor who recognize ancestral descent only through one side of the family. A matrilineage is a lineage whose members are descended through the female line. Most lineages are corporate or "legal" units holding land and other resources in common, settling grievances, collaborating in labor, sharing food and so on. She reasoned that Dinnebito phase villages would be composed of a lineage because of their size, the fact that there is no motive for unrelated families to band together, and because lineages form communities for most societies around the world at this level of social and economic complexity. The existence of a matrilineage is inferred from the fact that the Hopi villages today are composed of matrilineages, which tend to be the typical descent and corporate group structure for sedentary, low productivity agricultural societies with minimal social stratification.

Chandler feels that the shifts from subsurface to surface dwellings, from isolated to contiguous structures, and from circular to rectangular dwellings, relate to one another and to changes in social organization. She points out that surface rooms and rectangular rooms can be physically joined together and that this reflects the existence of cooperative social units.

Figure 5.10. Az. D:7:134, plan view of the site. Various tests using ceramic design analysis suggested the order in which the site was occupied and then abandoned.

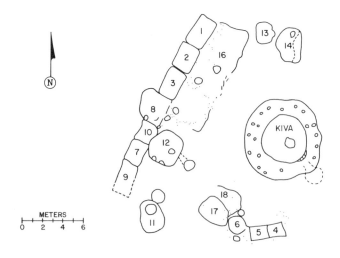

The social relationship of the three closely spaced Dinnebito villages is difficult to determine. Using the few available tree-ring dates, ceramic analysis, and the similarity in corn types (suggesting little evolutionary development), Chandler believes the three villages are at least partly contemporaneous. The question then is, did the three villages function as a single community? If indeed the individual villages consisted of a matrilineage, there are real advantages to having other matrilineal villages in the vicinity. Each village consisting of a female-related line must find husbands from other villages, and males tend to marry women in nearby communities so that close ties with their own matrilineages can be maintained. There is female residence and descent, but male authority and ceremonial responsibilities; so while it is necessary to have men marry into a different village, it is also important that their home village be close by. This enables the men to carry on their responsibilities to their own matrilineage as well as to the village into which they married.

Obviously these discussions of social relationships are based on a great deal of speculation. Inferences are made about human social relationships from the shape of dwellings, their distance from one another, and the distance of sites from one another.

Analogies are made from the Hopi, the direct, living descendants of the Dinnebito people, and from other peoples all over the world who seemingly possess many of the social and economic characteristics of the Dinnebito phase Anasazi.

Little can be said about Dinnebito interaction with other cultures off the mesa that has not been said already about the cultures of other phases on Black Mesa. Exotic items such as shell, which were obtained on long-distance collecting trips or by exchange with traders, are neither more nor less frequent than during other phases. Ceramic design similarity with other Kayenta areas indicates shared style and perhaps trading within the region.

Wepo Phase (Pueblo I–Pueblo II), A.D. *975 to 1050*

The Wepo phase seems to have been a major turning point in the cultural history of Black Mesa. Population increased dramatically. Favored living locations were along washes and upland basins that could be used for farming. A number of Wepo phase sites, including two that were excavated, were located on a long terrace off the north escarpment of the mesa where runoff collects.

The Wepo phase Anasazi may have relied more on hunting and gathering than their predecessors. Preliminary evidence suggests that during the Wepo phase the percentage of maize decreased in relation to cactus seeds, grass, and weeds. Furthermore, projectile points, presumably used for hunting, while always somewhat scarce on Black Mesa, are more abundant than in any other period. The high incidence of projectile points, however, rather than indicating more hunting during this period, may be a result of the location of Wepo phase sites on the northern terrace of Black Mesa, an area closer to a source of stone excellent for chipping. Stone for making high quality chipped points is not readily available on Black Mesa. Furthermore, many southwestern people did not always use stone arrowheads, but simply sharpened the wooden shaft of the arrow, so no trace is left of these hunting implements, except in dry caves. In short, the apparently larger number of projectile points during the Wepo phase may be a result of the fact that during other periods hunters used more sharpened sticks for arrows, which have subsequently disintegrated, or Wepo phase sites closer to good stone sources were chosen for excavation. Botanical evidence showing a decrease in corn and an increase in wild plant food, however, corresponds with the possibility of an increased emphasis on hunting.

Climate studies may provide the answer for this apparent reversion from a more intensive agricultural economy to increased hunting and gathering. Evidence from tree rings and from surface geology indicates a slight shift to a cooler and wetter climate at the end of the Dinnebito phase and the beginning of the Wepo phase. Crops may have failed, occasionally due to a shorter growing season as the result of late spring and early fall frosts. This situation would require a more diverse subsistence base. The magnitude of climatic changes and the cultural responses to these changes are extremely difficult to determine even though Black Mesa provides one of the most precise case studies for the relationship between culture and environmental change.

Ceramics, as might be expected, are one of the indicators of change and experimentation during the Wepo phase. The black-on-white decorated pottery continues its slow but steady evolution of painted style design. It is the utilitarian gray ware that for the first and only time in Anasazi culture history shows real evidence of freedom of expression and experimentation. The gray ware of the Dinnebito phase, used mainly for cooking (as evidenced by the amount of smoke blacking on the exterior) is very rough surfaced.

Around the neck of jars are coils which are not obliterated, but which are flattened. During the Wepo phase the necks of jars were manipulated in a number of ways while the clay was still wet. The coils were sometimes obliterated and a sharp instrument used to produce horizontal, closely spaced grooves, creating a fluted effect. Many varieties of this decoration are common. Circles, checkerboards, chevrons, and point patterns are incised into the neck. Even fingernails were used to produce a series of half moon incisions. In some cases, clay was applied in small lumps or lines to the neck of the vessel to create high relief decoration. One form of neck decoration presages the later utility wares. The coils on the neck were deeply indented in a regular and carefully executed pattern. Often fingerprints can be seen in the clay. The decorated area has an even, wavy, corrugated pattern. In some cases during the Wepo phase, the corrugating effect went halfway down onto the body of the jar, stopping at the widest diameter of the vessel. During the next phase (Lamoki) and in Pueblo II, throughout the Anasazi country the entire vessel was corrugated. This type is known to archaeologists as Tusayan Corrugated.

The interest in the variation in plain ware vessels is not simply a concern for the evolution of design style or even for the use of ceramics as a dating tool. A number of technical and behavioral questions have been asked about gray ware ceramic evolution. Unfortunately none of these questions has been answered.

Most of the designs on the necks of Wepo phase vessels are just that—design. Why, however, should this period produce such a wide variety of design, and why should it be executed on the plain and, at least to our modern eye, aesthetically uninteresting vessels rather than the beautiful painted containers?

While most archaeologists feel that the transition in unpainted ceramics from Kana-a Gray to Tusayan Corrugated is purely stylistic, other archaeologists have suggested functional interpretations. The indented and corrugated extension of a vessel has considerably more surface area than does a smooth-surfaced vessel and consequently should conduct heat better. A corrugated vessel would heat up quickly and reduce cooking time, a sort of prehistoric microwave oven. This explanation is doubtful, however, since the corrugations first were used on the neck of the jar, an area not placed over the fire and not necessary for conducting heat. Another suggestion is that the corrugation provided a surer grip which would be effective on the larger vessels, especially when they were full.

The configuration of Wepo phase sites is similar to that of Dinnebito phase sites. Some villages tend toward the formal Anasazi pattern, while others are a hodgepodge clustering of structures with no apparent plan. The structures also vary tremendously in form. They may be large or small, rectangular or circular, and made of jacal, masonry, or a combination of the two. One dwelling was found with a masonry wall against a large boulder, another wall composed of upright slabs, and the remaining two walls made of masonry interspersed with jacal!

Storage rooms were large, unlined, rectangular or oval pits. One pit had a surface masonry wall extending almost a meter above the old ground surface.

Kivas constructed during this phase showed more formal characteristics. Often they were masonry lined and plastered with a light gray or brown clay. Sometimes a hole about a meter long and 20 centimeters wide, cut in a V-shape 15 to 20 centimeters deep, was placed in the floor between the hearth and back wall. Since these holes are unlined and their shape would prevent them from being effective storage pits, they may have been foot drums, features found in modern kivas (Fig. 5.11). Boards are placed over pits in the floor so that when dancers rhythmically stamp on them during their performances a loud thumping is produced.

No unique spatial relationship has been noticed among Wepo phase sites. Clustering as observed in the Dinnebito phase sites is unapparent, neither do there appear to be sites of widely varying sizes or functions. Certainly hunting camps and the like were established, but they have not been recorded on survey.

One reason specialized activity sites may not have been recognized, according to Shirley Powell, is that *all* Wepo phase sites in the lease area were used seasonally. To test her hypothesis she turned to the methods of ethnoarchaeology, using data from recently abandoned Navajo sites on Black Mesa.

Powell thought that by examining differences in site size, hearth locations, and artifact density she could determine the season in which the site was occupied. Given a similar population at any location, summer-occupied sites should have less interior and more exterior space, much as modern houses in warm-weather areas have large pool-patio-barbeque complexes, while homes in colder climates have more space devoted to dens and recreation rooms. Hearth location as an indication of seasonality is based on the logical notion that in winter-occupied sites hearths will be situated inside to provide warmth; in summer structures hearths, used for cooking, not for heating, will be outside. Powell postulated that summer-occupied sites would have the same number of artifacts as winter sites but that they would be scattered over a larger area because of summer outdoor living. Artifacts in winter sites would be concentrated in a smaller space because much activity would take place inside.

In historic times the Navajo have located their summer settle-

Figure 5.11. A kiva with manos and metates on the floor (upper left) and an oval foot drum (center), which would have been covered with a board, near the hearth.

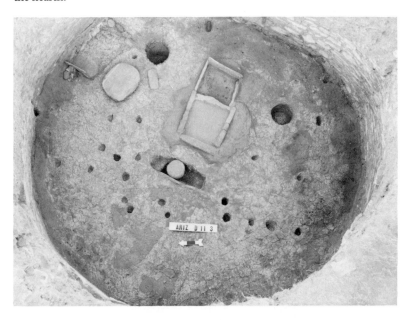

ments near major agricultural fields and their winter communities away from the fields in areas better suited for hunting, wild plant and nut collecting, and storage. By interviewing Navajos who had friends and relatives who actually used the sites, Powell was able to establish their function and to measure the variables, such as site size, that she wished to test. Structures at summer sites were, as she had postulated, significantly smaller. Exterior hearths were more frequent than interior ones, and artifacts were more widely scattered than in winter occupations.

The next step in the analysis was to test these ethnographic "truths" on the archaeological record. Amazingly, all the Anasazi sites in her sample had interior space of less than 12 or more than 17.2 square meters. They were either large or small and clustered according to the amount of enclosed space they had; there were, in effect, no medium-size sites. Hearth placement and artifact density were as predicted: smaller enclosed areas had fewer interior hearths and less densely spaced artifacts, and larger enclosed areas had more hearths and artifacts were more concentrated.

Because Navajo summer sites were located near large agricultural fields, Shirley predicted that Anasazi summer sites would cluster along the major washes near the better agricultural land and winter sites would be located in the uplands of Black Mesa. This was not the case, however.

Since the Wepo phase and earlier sites all fit the summer settlement characteristics, Powell believes that the lease area was only occupied during the summer. She detects both seasonal occupation and year-round settlements following the Wepo phase. Where people lived in winter during those earlier phases is not known, but it may well have been nearby, possibly in the valley off the north edge of Black Mesa or the central part of the mesa itself.

While the distinction between seasonal and permanent occupations may not be as distinct as Powell has postulated, she has demonstrated that a great deal more seasonal movement occurred than previously thought. From what is known ethnographically about mixed hunting-gathering and semi-agricultural groups, her findings make sense.

The first burials found on Black Mesa date to the Wepo phase, and although the sample is small, they hint at mortuary customs. Mortuary practices are usually rigidly defined by custom. Throughout the Southwest, archaeologists have plotted the distribution of burial practices. Some people cremated their dead, such as the Hohokam of southern Arizona, while in other areas people buried their dead extended or in a position with legs flexed and knees near the chest.

Like most Anasazi, the Black Mesa people preferred to bury their dead in trash heaps, a custom most of us find irreverent, to say the least. The standard archaeological explanation has been that the Anasazi had only sticks with which to dig, and excavating a grave in a soft trash heap made more sense than digging in undisturbed consolidated soil.

Many of the Black Mesa burials have been so badly disturbed by dogs or other animals, and the bones so poorly preserved, that it is impossible to determine the orientation of the body. A Wepo phase burial and several others from later periods were placed in an unusual position. The body was set upright with legs crossed in what used to be called tailor fashion. The arms were folded with the hands in the lap. Because of the upright position, the rib cage had collapsed and the cranium had fallen off the spinal column. The hole in which the body was placed was very small. In the Wepo phase and later periods, funerary furniture was sparse, usually only worn or broken vessels.

We find little evidence of trade or contact with outside groups in the Wepo phase sites. One exception may be the style of some pithouses excavated at one site. They are shallow and rectangular, and their entryways were constructed by cutting a narrow ramp from the ground surface to the floor of the structure. This pithouse form is common for the Mogollon in the mountains of Arizona south of Black Mesa. Rather than postulate a "southern connection" for this architectural style, however, it is easier to explain the entry form as an adaptation to a shallow pithouse where a roof entry would be less practical. The shallowness of the structures may be a compromise between a surface and subsurface structure, and the many forms of architecture may be a result of experimentation.

Lamoki Phase (Early Pueblo II), A.D. 1050 to 1100

The Pueblo II period was a time of great geographical expansion for the Anasazi. Thousands of Pueblo II sites dot areas that previously had been sparsely inhabited. Often these newly inhabited areas were uplands, away from the major stream channels in generally cooler and drier environments. During this period the Virgin and Winslow traditions of the Anasazi reached their peak, although they never approached the site density, size, or apparent sophistication of the Chaco, Mesa Verde, and Kayenta traditions. This expansion of area during Pueblo II usually has been attributed to a more favorable climate and a corresponding population increase.

Pueblo II in the Kayenta area is distinguished by a trend to above-ground masonry or jacal structures often with a village plan so rigid that the sites look as if they were made with a cookie cutter. The typical pattern is a row of contiguous above-ground dwellings with a subsurface kiva in front and a trash midden on the other side of the kiva.

In some parts of the Mesa Verde and Chaco areas the Anasazi were congregating in large towns and were developing societies dependent on economic specialization, trade for luxury goods, and status differentiations among different segments of the population. There is some suggestion that a society dominated by religious leaders may have been developing. During this time the large communities of Mesa Verde and Chaco Canyon flourished with their extensive irrigation systems, complex religious structure, and, in the Chaco area, a long and sophisticated system of roads. Clearly these two Anasazi areas were part of a regional network that permitted and encouraged cultural development exceeding that of the Kayenta area.

On Black Mesa the early Pueblo II period is known as the Lamoki phase. During this phase in some parts of the Peabody lease area population levels reached their maximum. It was also the period of maximum settlement in the upland regions. All types of environmental niches were occupied, including for the first and only time, the shallow caves and cliff shelters at the extreme northeast edge of the mesa. While they do not compare in number, size, quality of construction, or grandeur to the famous cliff dwellings in national parks and monuments, they are nevertheless true cliff dwellings. These sites are at the extreme elevations of the mesa in an environment of scrub oak, Douglas-fir, aspen, and ponderosa pine.

During the Lamoki phase, relatively large villages not con-

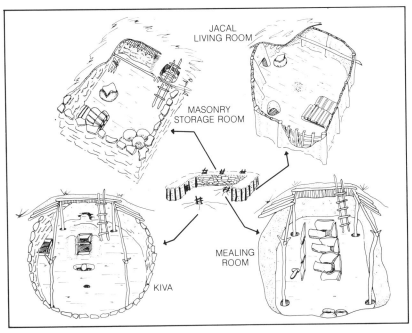

Figure 5.12. An idealized Lamoki site plan with a row of masonry storage rooms in back with two connecting jacal wings of dwellings, a kiva, and a corn mealing room

strained in their shape by walls or cliffs, took on a more formal orientation. The prototypical village (Fig. 5.12) had a row of masonry rooms with a series of contiguous jacal rooms extending at right angles from the ends of the masonry room block. In the center of the U-shaped group of rooms was the kiva (Fig. 5.13). Almost invariably there was a specialized subsurface room for the mealing of corn off the northeast corner of the masonry structure between the roomblock and the kiva (Fig. 5.14). The trash midden, often quite large and as much as a meter deep, was beyond the kiva. Encircling walls made of wooden posts which seem to encompass the entire site except for the midden, have been found in recent years at a number of these sites. Whether the walls were used as windbreaks, fences, or for defensive purposes is not known.

Variations on this basic village plan included sites with only jacal rooms, without mealing rooms, without kivas, with a single jacal room extension from the masonry roomblock, and almost every other conceivable modification.

Determining the functions of the various rooms has been the object of several Black Mesa studies, the most comprehensive of which is a master's thesis written by Kathy Bagley, an SIU student.

An understanding of room function is important for making inferences about demography, social organization, and subsistence activities. Population size is directly reflected by number and size of dwellings. Juxtaposition of dwellings to one another and to other room types, such as storage rooms and corn mealing rooms, can suggest certain forms of social organization. The identification of kiva attributes indicates certain types of communal sacred and secular activities. Size, shape, and remaining contents of storage rooms help determine what type and quantity of food was stored.

Figure 5.13. Excavating a kiva. Workers are standing on top of the collapsed roof and are uncovering burned beams.

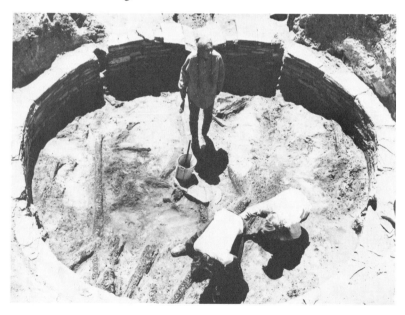

To determine room function, Bagley examined six different room features. For example, she looked at floor area assuming that storage areas would be smaller than dwellings. Hearths in a structure indicate it was used as a dwelling, and so on. As might be expected, her conclusion was that each type of room (masonry, jacal, or pithouse) was used for several different functions, but that generalizations can be made about each type. Masonry rooms usually were specialized storage structures. This function is inferred mainly from the absence of artifacts and features that would suggest a habitation function or specialized workroom. They do not, with only two exceptions, have hearths, and they tend to contain relatively few artifacts other than potsherds.

Pithouses, on the other hand, seem to have had a number of functions. They yield a great abundance of artifacts indicating they served as both habitation and storage rooms. They contain features that indicate activities such as cooking, eating, and grinding

Figure 5.14. A subsurface room for the mealing of corn. Metates (grinding stones) were placed in the slab-lined compartments. The roof and upper walls were constructed of wood and clay.

of food, as well as the manufacture of tools and the storage of food. The substructures classified as subsurface mealing rooms are characterized by an absence of hearths and by a number of slab-lined boxes in the floor which held metates.

Another study which tends to confirm Bagley's determination of room function was done by Shereen Lerner of Arizona State University. She attempted to determine the function of ceramic vessels based on their shape, then she compared the shapes with the types of rooms in which they were found. Her main concern was differentiating types of bowls and jars, assuming that the diameter of the vessel orifices and height of the neck determines the tasks for which the vessel was used. She distinguished seven functional classes based on orifice diameter and neck height measurements: 1) Cooking jars: Jars with wide orifices and open necks—or white wares; 2) Temporary or possibly long-term storage: Jars with medium orifice and restricted necks—gray wares and some white wares; 3) Temporary storage: Jars with wide orifices and restricted necks—gray ware or white wares; 4) Serving dishes: Bowls with medium orifices and medium necks—gray or white ware; 5) Temporary storage, serving, and a small amount of food preparation: Bowls with medium orifice and medium neck—gray ware or white ware; 6) Serving and eating: Bowls with wide orifice—white ware with large volume of flow; 7) Short-term containers, individualized serving possible: Bowls with small orifices and restricted necks, small volume of flow.

Using statistical techniques she examined ceramics from six sites. She found that jacal rooms contained vessels which were used predominantly for serving and food preparation or temporary storage, something to be expected of a habitation room. There was a very significant relationship between the occurrence of subsurface structures and the presence of black-on-white bowls used for serving food. Masonry rooms contained a preponderance of gray ware jars with a wide orifice and restricted height, reinforcing the notion that these rooms were used mainly for storage. Mealing rooms contained jars with simple necks and unrestricted orifices that fit the type of vessel postulated for food processing. In sum, the analysis of ceramic function confirmed the analysis of room function.

Parenthetically, the study of ceramic function also revealed that cooking jars became larger in the later phases while serving bowls remained the same size. This helps confirm the hypothesis that population was increasing through time. With increasingly large families, larger family cooking jars would be required, but individual serving bowls would, of course, remain the same because food portions would not be increased and in fact might even be smaller.

The question of why the different types of structures were used for different functions has not been adequately addressed, although there are several logical explanations. Masonry stops rodents from burrowing through walls to get at stored food. Sometimes the floors of masonry structures, and only masonry structures, were slab lined, presumably also to keep out rodents. That various animals got into the stored food is evidenced by a deep storage pit excavated at a Wepo phase site. An animal had dug a very large hole from the surface of the ground about 75 cm deep into the unlined wall of the pit. After the robbery was discovered, the hole was blocked up with masonry.

Jacal is easier to construct than masonry, therefore when the advantages of masonry were not needed, as in dwellings, jacal sufficed. While masonry lasts a long time, jacal lasts much longer than one would expect. The clay that is daubed over the wooden framework is often found in excavations, and fragments of the juniper posts are usually still in place. In some instances, the posts are so well preserved that they can be seen protruding above the surface. These are sawed off during survey in order to obtain tree-ring dates.

The only explanation for the existence of subsurface mealing rooms is that the wall of the excavated pit provided a solid surface against which the kneeling woman who was grinding corn could place her feet. According to Hopi women, this kneeling position with feet against a wall allows extra force to be applied on the mano which crushes the corn. A solid pit wall would provide a more solid backing than a jacal or masonry wall. The space between the mealing bins which held metates and the wall is always the appropriate distance to accommodate a kneeling person with feet against the wall.

The continued but only occasional use of pithouses for habitation throughout the later part of the Black Mesa sequence poses some interesting questions. At sites where pithouses are the only dwelling, they apparently served both habitation and storage functions, as Bagley's study suggests. Why pithouses at other sites are associated with surface masonry and jacal structures, used for storage and habitation, is not known.

During the Lamoki phase there was a sharp increase in the production of corn and a corresponding decrease in the consumption of wild plants. Paleoclimate reconstruction indicates a cooler, wetter climate at this time which probably permitted more successful agriculture and reduced the need for hunting and gathering.

Dried human feces, or coprolites, found in the cliff dwellings at the northeastern part of the mesa provide a unique opportunity for reconstructing the diet of the Lamoki phase Anasazi. They were examined for plant remains and pollen which can indicate the season they were formed and deposited.

All the specimens contained plant pollen available mainly in July and August, and therefore reflected that season's diet. Cultivated crops found were corn, beans, and squash with corn most heavily represented. Since these crops do not ripen until September and October at high elevations, they were probably stored from the previous year. Juniper charcoal was also found, suggesting that the corn kernels may have been parched. Pueblo Indians historically roast the kernels by shaking them in a clay-lined basket with live coals. That this was one method of cooking is suggested also by the recovery in the coprolites of some whole, partially burned kernels.

Beans are rarely found archaeologically because they do not have the tough exterior of corn or the rind of squash. Probably the only reason a bean was found in the coprolites was because it was swallowed whole without being chewed. Surprisingly, both squash seeds and rinds were part of the diet.

The wild foods which were consumed included groundcherry, fishhook and prickly pear cactus fruits, and possibly pigweed or lambsquarters.

Along with an increase in agricultural production in the Lamoki phase, a more efficient storage and food distribution network may have developed, perhaps even a site which was used specifically for this purpose. The largest and most spectacular cliff dwelling is known as Standing Fall House. The fifty-five-room ruin has hundreds of corn cobs scattered in virtually every room and courtyard (Fig. 5.15). This is not unusual, however, in the protected environment of the cliff. What is unusual for this large site is the scarcity of potsherds in and around the ruin and the absence of a trash midden either under the cliff overhang or at the base of the cliff. This may mean that Standing Fall House was occupied for a very short time or that the site served some special purpose and was not a habitation site. Tony Klesert decided the key to determining site function was determining the function of the individual rooms. Using several methods for determining room function, he found that approximately 78 percent of the site was used for storage and the rest consisted of dwellings and two kivas. This ratio of storage space to dwelling space is highly unusual, not only for Black Mesa but for other Anasazi areas as well. Because of the large percentage of storage facilities and the slight evidence for habitation in the form of dwellings and the lack of a

Figure 5.15. A kiva at Standing Fall House with three roof timbers still in place

garbage midden, he concluded that Standing Fall House was used primarily as an intercommunity storage center for people living at other villages in the vicinity. The presence of kivas at the site suggests that Standing Fall House may have served not only as an economic center, but also as a center of social and religious activity for the population which was scattered over the northeastern part of the mesa. Klesert's arguments are not completely convincing, but the idea of centralized storage and distribution of parts of the food supply is worth testing further because of its tremendous social implications.

Possibly during the Lamoki phase and certainly by the Toreva phase the Black Mesa subsistence base definitely had changed, largely in the kinds of animals being hunted and eaten. During the entire Black Mesa phase sequence, the ratio of rabbits, both cottontail and jackrabbits, to rodents remained about 3 to 1. The ratio of large mammals, deer, and mountain sheep to rabbits dropped from 1 to 3.5 in the Wepo phase, to an incredible 1 to 73 by the Toreva phase! Several possible explanations exist for the sharp decrease in large mammals in the diet.

It cannot be assumed simply that dietary preference changed, because individual deer and mountain sheep produce so much protein and fat in comparison to rabbits that it is unreasonable to assume this meat source would be ignored if it was available. More likely, large animals simply were not as abundant because they were being overhunted by the expanding population. Furthermore the population movement to the uplands and the greater amount of land under cultivation might well have partially displaced the mountain sheep. Another partial explanation for the decrease in the hunting of large mammals might be the increased emphasis on agriculture. The best time for hunting deer is in the fall when much labor is needed for the harvest.

As any youngster with a pet male and female rabbit can attest, rabbits reproduce rapidly and, if overhunted, can quickly regain their numbers. Such is not the case with deer and mountain sheep. It takes a number of years to reestablish a depleted population. Attempts to reestablish a deer herd on Black Mesa a few years ago proved largely unsuccessful because a deer seen is soon a deer shot and eaten.

Another poorly understood hint of change in the subsistence economy is the way in which food was prepared. Prior to the Lamoki phase, slab-lined roasting pits were common. These were as deep as 3 feet and sometimes had several layers of ash, each separated by a horizontal sandstone slab, as if they were several layered ovens. These roasting pits are seldom found in sites post-dating the Wepo phase. Whether they represent a change in diet or simply a change in food preparation is unknown.

Another change in food preparation was the switch from the use of basin metates and two-hand manos to the built-in mealing bin with a flat metate, a much more efficient means of grinding the corn and collecting the meal. The increasing reliance on corn may have required more energy-efficient means of processing the food.

While many of these conclusions about subsistence and food preparation are based on preliminary studies and sometimes on scanty evidence, they do add up to a picture of a variation in the types of food eaten from phase to phase. When it came to eating, the Black Mesa Anasazi had to be expedient.

Toreva Phase (Late Pueblo II), A.D. *1100 to 1150*

The Toreva phase marked the peak as well as the decline of the Anasazi occupation on northern Black Mesa. Minor shifts in settlement location are apparent during this phase which perhaps have something to do with climatic fluctuations.

By the Lamoki phase the eastern part of the coal lease area had reached its maximum population, while it appears that the largest population in the western lease area was during the Toreva phase. It must be remembered that the eastern and western coal leases are contiguous in places, and never more than ten miles apart which means population displacements occurred over very slight distances. While the environments of the eastern and western lease areas seem superficially similar, on closer examination it is evident that small variations would affect primitive agriculturalists. The major difference between the eastern and western lease areas is elevation. Much of the eastern lease area is 6,800 feet or more

Figure 5.16. A Toreva phase site with kiva in foreground, masonry storage rooms in back and, unseen, disintegrated post- and clay-constructed dwelling rooms on each end of the storage structure

above sea level. A number of scholars have pointed out that 6,800 feet is a critical elevation throughout much of the Southwest because above it the growing season tends to be too short and crops are ruined by frost before they reach maturity. Today, the Navajos on Black Mesa do not grow much besides potatoes and alfalfa above this elevation because of frost danger. Evidence suggests that much of the eastern lease area was occupied during the warmer Lamoki phase and the early part of the Toreva. As the summer growing season became shorter later in the Toreva phase, it was necessary to move to the west where the danger of frost was less severe.

Site configuration during the Toreva phase remains much the same as in the Lamoki phase, but a number of Toreva sites with apparently different functions have been investigated, permitting greater speculation about the relationships of different types of sites to one another (Figure 5.16). The different types of sites have been seen as expressions of variations in social organization, as a result of differences in function, and as a reflection of seasonal occupation. These explanations are not, of course, mutually exclusive, and, in fact, a combination of the three seems the most logical alternative.

The first attempt at an explanation for different types of contemporary sites was an ingenious scheme proposed by Dave Phillips while still an undergraduate at Prescott College. He saw the major variation in Toreva phase site types as a result of population pressure and the expansion of population into the uplands. He suggested that when the population was small and concentrated along the major drainages, individual communities were relatively autonomous primarily because critical resources, particularly land and water, were evenly distributed. As the population grew, however, it became necessary to cultivate somewhat less desirable upland areas; to avoid long walks from fields to villages, people constructed habitation sites in the uplands. The movement to the higher land, however, was not accomplished without considerable adjustment in social organization to adapt to the shift from a lineal settlement pattern along the drainages to a pattern of widely scattered villages in the uplands. Phillips suggested that this movement resulted in two types of sites: the mother site and the daughter site. The first site type was a relatively autonomous U-shaped village consisting of dwellings, storage facilities, kivas, and subsurface mealing rooms. Daughter sites were smaller, had dwellings and storage rooms, but no kivas. Phillips believes that daughter sites were not seasonally occupied nor were they used for special purposes such as hunting. He suggests that the large number of small sites scattered over the uplands permitted villages to be situated close to many small pockets of arable land.

While the function of the daughter sites was primarily an economic one, the mother site with its kiva was the location for the renewal of social and religious ties.

An attempt was made by Bob Clemen, then a Stanford University undergraduate, to understand the social organization of the mother site, which might shed some light on the process of site expansion. A number of years ago several southwestern archaeologists attempted to discover the existence of matrilineages at a large prehistoric pueblo. They assumed, using the Hopi as a model, that the inhabitants were both matrilocal and matrilineal, that is, the husbands went to live with the wives, and descent was reckoned through the female line. They also assumed, as is true with the Hopi today, that the women were the potters. If these assumptions were correct, they reasoned that mothers taught their married daughters, who lived with them, how to make ceramics, passing on certain traditions which should be reflected in the sherds found in localized parts of the pueblo. These archaeologists knew that standard ceramic types were too general to reflect the nuances in ceramic design needed to test their hypothesis, so they worked with ceramic design elements, somewhat like those the Black Mesa project used for relative dating. While the pioneering efforts were afflicted with some problems, they did reveal statistically significant clustering of design elements in different parts of the pueblo.

Clemen tried this technique on a Toreva phase site. The results are shown in Figure 5.17. Some of the rooms were disturbed by heavy equipment prior to excavation, and in some cases the paucity of sherds created statistical problems. Nevertheless, the study suggests that a matrilineage may have occupied each jacal wing, with mothers passing the nuances of painting ceramic designs on to their daughters. As might be expected, the mealing room con-

Figure 5.17. Site plan showing the spatial relationship of certain ceramic design styles. The mealing room shared design elements with both jacal wings 1 and 2, and masonry room 1 is associated with jacal wing 1.

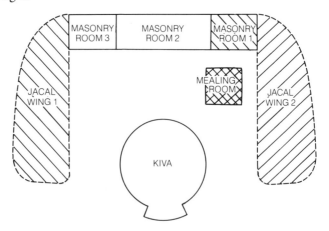

tained ceramics with designs typical of both jacal wings, indicating that the room was used for communal work. If this is indeed the social organization of the mother site, the composition of daughter sites is probably the result of one of the matrilineages expanding in size; the "surplus" population of one jacal wing may have budded off to form a new settlement close to good agricultural land, but returned to the mother village for certain socioreligious activities.

Smaller Toreva phase sites also may have been used for special purposes and only temporarily occupied. Mark Catlin of SIU wrote his master's thesis testing this hypothesis.

To demonstrate that certain sites were used for functionally specific purposes such as hunting or plant collecting, it is necessary to show that the environment being exploited was not homogenous. If the resources were evenly distributed over the landscape, the Anasazi would have had no need to travel far and wide setting up special camps for food collecting and processing.

There is, indeed, clear differentiation between environmental zones on Black Mesa. The most obvious is the difference between the piñon-juniper woodlands and the sagebrush-covered flats. The piñon-juniper woodland is located along the tops and slopes of hills and ridges. This is not good agricultural land because the soil is thin and very rocky, and moisture is quickly lost through runoff. Sagebrush covers the alluvium-filled drainages and basins. This suggests that the necessary water and soil for successful farming occurred in the present dry sage zones. The woodlands area, while not suitable for agriculture, had an important economic function, for it yielded many wild plant foods, especially the plentiful and nutritious piñon nut. Ethnographic evidence tells us that some southwestern Indians sent collecting parties into wooded areas to establish temporary camps specifically to harvest the piñon crop.

Given the fact that natural resources are localized, what evidence is there that different types of sites and artifacts for different functions cluster in the different environmental zones? Using both surveyed and excavated sites, Catlin first looked for differences in site features and defined two types of sites. The first type had no definite roomblocks, distinct kiva depressions, or trash midden, relatively few artifacts were found and it was 100 square meters or less in size. The second type had one or more roomblocks, kiva depressions, trash middens, a relatively large number of artifacts, and a size of 1,000 square meters or more. Catlin believes that sites of the second type were permanent habitation sites. They show evidence of long-term occupation and obviously permitted the full range of activities necessary to maintain a cultural system. Furthermore, analysis of floral and faunal remains indicates a wide variety of foodstuffs, demonstrating that many different subsistence activities were undertaken there.

The other sites probably were used temporarily and for a limited range of activities because of the small amount of residue and the absence of permanent dwellings, storage space, and kivas. Often, no structural features are found other than hearths. This type of site also shows a high degree of diversity of wild plant remains, but only a limited variety of animal bones, suggesting they were wild plant collecting stations. Catlin assumed that the permanent habitation sites were associated with agricultural activities and would be found near sagebrush zones and that the limited activity sites would be in the woodlands.

To test his assumptions he measured the percentage of the environment containing sagebrush within 0.5 kilometer of the sites and grouped the vegetation within the boundary of the site into three categories: woodland, transition, and sagebrush. He then statistically compared the large and small sites with the different environmental zones and found a very significant correlation between large habitation sites and the sage and transition zones, and between small, limited activity sites and the woodland zone. The permanent sites were associated with arable land. More specialized sites were situated in environments closely related to the subsistence activities being practiced. It makes good economic sense to construct a permanent village near fields which need tending during much of the year and to build temporary shelters near resources that can be exploited for only a short period.

Another test done by Margie Green tends to confirm the functional differences of sites of different sizes. Stone suitable for chipping is rare on Black Mesa. The local stone used for tools is sandstone, siderite, siltstone, quartzite, and a granular petrified wood—the poorest quality material. The chippable stone found off the mesa, but within 30 miles of the project area, is chert and limestone. The best material, found more than 30 miles from the area, is chert, obsidian, jasper, chalcedony, and a glassy petrified wood. In many cases, it is possible to determine the sources of stone tool material by physical and chemical composition. This technique is very useful in determining trade and travel networks and has been used extensively in Europe and Mesoamerica.

In this test, the type and amount of stone on the surface of sites were compared with site size. Green assumed that the stone indigenous to Black Mesa would be found at all sites in large quantities, while the more exotic stone would be found in larger proportions at larger habitation sites, because exotic stone would first be taken to a larger site where it would be chipped into tools, leaving substantial amounts of waste. The finished tools would then be transported to more specialized smaller sites. Since local materials were readily available, the waste materials and artifacts made of this stone should be found equally at all types of sites. When a specific tool type was needed, the material would be picked up and rapidly fashioned into a tool, leaving large amounts of chipping debris. Furthermore, she hypothesized that when exotic stone was found at smaller, limited activity sites, it would be in the form of finished artifacts rather than as waste from tool manufacture.

She somewhat arbitrarily classified the surveyed sites into five groups, depending on size and the presence or absence of surface features. She assumed that site size reflected social complexity with the smallest, least structurally complex sites being limited activity sites and the larger ones with more visible surface structures being habitation sites. Her preliminary results indicate that the abundance of artifacts of locally available raw material does not vary significantly at sites of different sizes, nor does there seem to be any relationship of site size to the percentage of finished tools. There is, however, a great variation in the amount of chipped stone in sites of different sizes. The smallest, least complex sites have significantly higher densities of local materials than do the larger communities. Also, materials from off the mesa but within 30 miles of it, are found in much greater abundance as site size and complexity increase. The stone from the most distant sources is most abundant at the larger sites.

If Green's hypotheses about the use and distribution of local and exotic chipped stone are correct, they would tend to confirm the distinction among site function proposed by Mark Catlin on the basis of distance from arable land.

Some sites may have been specialized food storage and preparation centers serving a group of permanent habitation sites. In 1968 a Toreva phase site was excavated which consisted of three contiguous masonry rooms with no kiva and no jacal structures. None of the rooms had hearths and two were devoid of any internal features. The third room had eight mealing bins which totally filled the floor area. Since there were no dwelling facilities at the site, it appears that this location was used solely for grinding and storing corn, perhaps for a single village, but more likely for several.

The tests on site function are necessary confirmation of what may seem intuitively obvious: that is, that people preferred to live close to their work and that relatively larger sites were used for more permanent year-long habitation, while small sites were what they seem—temporary camps.

Since these were rational people, they located both permanent and temporary sites where they would be most convenient for their subsistence activities—no long commutes for them if it proved economically unreasonable. Nevertheless, tests of the seemingly obvious are necessary if archaeologists are ever going to put their profession on a more solid scientific footing.

The concept of permanent habitation site versus special-use site does not, however, account for all the variation in Toreva phase site configuration. For example, a site was chosen for excavation in 1969 because it was a small sherd area with no surface structures visible. On excavation, the site was found to consist of two shallow, almost miniature pithouses, a one-room jacal structure, and a very small kiva. One of the rectangular pithouses measured less than 2 meters on a side. Why such a small site would have a kiva associated with it is unknown, but it should not be surprising that all sites do not fit into real functional or stylistic categories. While the vast majority of modern single family houses are churned out by builders using a set formula, some houses are architect designed and are decidedly different.

Unquestionably, site type and location are affected by the subsistence economy of Black Mesa, and the economy apparently changed slightly during the Toreva phase. Preliminary evidence suggests that the amount of corn being consumed decreased in relation to the amount of wild plant food, primarily grasses, especially during the later part of the Toreva phase prior to abandonment. The reason for this shift in the subsistence base is not well understood, especially since it may have taken place before the onset of a dry cycle which eventually contributed to the abandonment of the northeastern part of the mesa.

The trade relationship of the people on Black Mesa to one another and to their neighbors during the Toreva phase is a little clearer than for earlier periods. The preliminary study of lithic source identification by Margie Green has been described already. The techniques of constituent analysis she used can help identify sources of clays as well as minerals. The object of constituent analysis is to identify unique chemical characteristics specific to a particular source.

A common technique is thin section analysis, where a very thin slice of ceramic material containing stone and clay particles is mounted on a microscope slide. Many of the minerals in the clay are transparent, permitting source identification by identifying their constituents.

On Black Mesa a group of early pottery types called San Juan Red wares was tempered with a crushed volcanic rock. Since there are few sources of volcanic rock on Black Mesa, these vessels were probably imported. Tsegi Orange ware is another pottery type which did not occur on Black Mesa until the Toreva phase. These vessels were tempered with crushed potsherds. While their origin is not known, the introduction of Tsegi Orange ware on Black Mesa during the Toreva phase suggests an alteration in the pattern of social and economic interaction at this time.

One exciting new method for understanding exchange relationships between villages on and off the mesa is determining constituent analysis through neutron activation of the paste with which the vessels were constructed. Haree Deutchmann was a graduate student at SIU whose interest in neutron activation of ceramics and trade formed the basis of her doctoral dissertation. Her basic technique was to subject sherds from different sites to neutron activation to see if they were made of the same or different materials. She selected sherds from five neighboring sites on Black Mesa and from five at varying distances north of the mesa.

She chose contemporaneous Pueblo II sherds of two traditional types, Sosi Black-on-white and Dogoszhi Black-on-white, and analyzed them for iron, calcium, sodium, potassium, and eighteen trace elements such as cesium, barium, and scandium. What she found was that Black Mesa ceramics tend to cluster by site with two of the five sites having great similarity to each other in their ceramic paste composition. At one site, she found great differences in the paste composition between Sosi Black-on-white and Dogoszhi Black-on-white, and at another site there were major chemical differences between Sosi Black-on-white bowls and jars. Some of the ceramics seem to have very little chemical relationship to any others and finally, some of the sherds from off the mesa have a close relationship to some of the ceramics from sites on Black Mesa.

What do these results indicate? Because of the great similarity of paste composition at some sites, the ceramics probably came from the same source and were manufactured locally. The differences at one site between Sosi and Dogoszhi and at another between Sosi bowls and jars, suggest one pottery type and one shape of pottery came from different areas. The unique chemical makeup of some ceramics indicates trade from an unknown area, and the similarity of some sherds with non-Black Mesa sherds indicates trade between the two areas. The data suggest that much pottery was locally made in the villages and, in some instances, certain shapes and certain types may have been imported from both short and long distances.

These results are what might be expected, and yet certain cautionary statements have to be made. Some of these relationships are stronger than others, and even if results were unequivocal, alternative explanations to the trade hypothesis do exist. Potters from different villages may have used the same clay source, or potters from the same village may have selected different clays for different vessel shapes or design styles. Finally, the ceramics may not be exactly contemporaneous and different clay sources may have been used at slightly different times. All these factors may mask and alter relationships or be interpreted as the result of trade. Nevertheless, the study holds exciting prospects for better understanding of intervillage relationships or at the least, of intervillage potter relationships. No longer does similarity of design style

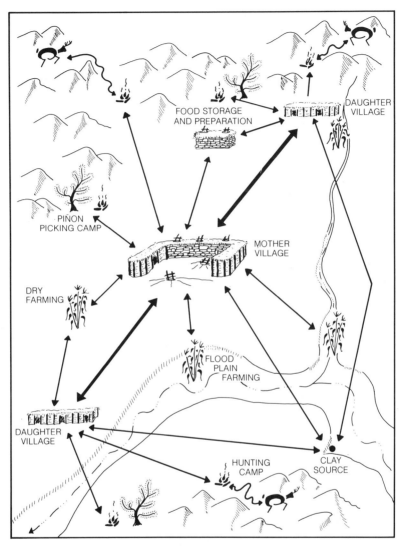

Figure 5.18. Various types of sites are integrated into a settlement system during the Toreva phase and reflect a community of interacting individuals.

imply equivalent paste nor are abundance of a single type and stylistic conformity criteria for local manufacture, an assumption often made by Southwesternists.

There is another hint of intervillage relationships, as Steve Plog has noted. Not all sites with kivas have associated masonry rooms. Some sites with kivas have only jacal rooms, or pithouses and storage pits. Those sites with kivas and masonry rooms, however, tend to have kivas that are larger, more elaborate in terms of internal features, and generally better constructed. He believes that sites with masonry storage rooms and larger kivas may have served as central storage and ceremonial areas for a group of smaller sites.

Finally, some of the smaller, more temporary Toreva phase sites may be the result of social disintegration prior to the abandonment of the northeastern part of Black Mesa. There is no evidence to suggest that some of these smaller temporary sites are later than the larger, permanent villages; however, they may represent temporary habitations for a few remaining families or a short, perhaps seasonal occupation for hunting and collecting after populations were relocated to the north and south (Fig. 5.18).

Completion of the Toreva phase marks the end of the prehistoric period within the boundaries of the Peabody Coal Company lease area. With the Navajo entry into the region by at least the late 1800s, a new, different and historical cultural sequence begins. The termination of the Anasazi sequence in the lease area does not, however, mean the end of the entire Anasazi sequence, but rather the need arises to focus attention outside the lease area to understand the continuously unfolding drama of Anasazi culture history.

6

Movement, Change, and the Clash of Cultures

FTER THE TOREVA PHASE, when the Anasazi left the lease area, the cultural landscape needs to be painted with a broader brush, since archaeologists do not have the luxury of the detailed analysis afforded by contract funds from Peabody Coal Company. Therefore, the scale of questions and interpretations must be adjusted to the quality and quantity of available data. But what intriguing questions—large-scale abandonment, population movements, and the introduction into the region of different cultures.

ABANDONMENT

The process of abandonment has fascinated archaeologists, historians, and laymen for generations. The mystery and excitement of decline and fall, abandonment and overthrow, are heightened by the possibility of cataclysmic events, moral decay, and by our desire to detect cycles or forces which may affect our own civilization.

Abandonment traditionally has been thought to be the result of some specific set of circumstances, often with a direct impact on the population. Burned areas of cities in the Near East have been viewed as the handiwork of conquering hordes who put the area to the torch. Heavy alluvial deposits over an occupation have been interpreted as evidence of a great natural catastrophe. Such interpretations often are simple attempts to explain complicated demographic situations. But single-cause explanations are usually doomed to failure; witness the many alternative hypotheses proposed for the disintegration of the Roman Empire. Most archaeologists and historians today view population movements and depopulation as the result of many direct and indirect social and environmental factors.

A major problem facing any archaeologist trying to understand abandonment is determining the basic facts: where did the people live and when did they go? After these questions have been answered, a host of others can be raised. Is this a case of decreasing birth or increasing death rates, or both? Or, was population actually increasing when, for whatever reasons, people moved away? Temporal control, as imprecise as it usually is in archaeology, often presents a picture of rapid abandonment, but it may have been gradual or it may have proceeded at varying rates. Simple concordances of climatic fluctuations or food availability with large-scale population movement does not constitute proof of the causality of the relationship, but even more importantly does not help us understand the human dynamics of the abandonment process. How do people under stress act before, during, and after the decision to move is made?

The abandonment of northern Black Mesa about A.D. 1150 was not an isolated incident. It reflected a general movement of population from the upland areas of the Colorado Plateau, which had been inhabited first in Pueblo II times.

One explanation is that nomadic raiders or enemy peoples arrived in the northern Southwest at this time. The evidence cited for this invasion is the increasingly defensive nature of sites postdating A.D. 1150, and the knowledge that Athabascans (Navajo and Apache) as well as Ute and Southern Paiute extended their range into Anasazi country sometime before the arrival of the Spaniards.

Some sites were constructed on easily defensible prominences and had high barricade-like walls, maze-like entryways, and even wall slits like those in medieval castles. It is difficult for a visitor at Mesa Verde National Park, climbing down a ladder to a cliff dwelling and squeezing into a narrow entryway, not to conclude that the site was constructed to keep unwanted people out. Intuitively, these "defensive" sites, along with some burned sites and very rare evidence of cannibalism, suggest that warfare was an important factor in the population movement. The warfare hypothesis, however, has not been tested rigorously. The Anasazi always utilized cliff shelters and seldom is there evidence in burial populations of violent, man-inflicted death.

There is historical evidence of nomadic raiding against the Pueblos. The sedentary villagers with their storage coffers full of corn and other domesticates provided a tempting target for the more mobile Navajo and Apache raiders who only occasionally grew crops. Spanish accounts are rife with Pueblo complaints of continual Navajo harrassment and raiding of settlements for food, especially sheep, which were compatible with the nomadic Navajo lifeway.

Proponents of the "enemy people" theory, however, have to contend with archaeological and linguistic evidence that indicates that the Navajo and Apache probably did not enter the Anasazi country until just before the arrival of the Spaniards, sometime before A.D. 1500. Pueblo ceramics occasionally have been found in direct contact with Southern Paiute sherds, but most archaeologists and linguists feel that the Southern Paiute and Ute were still in the Great Basin of Nevada and not in the Four Corners area until at least A.D. 1300.

There is also the possibility of internecine warfare—brother against brother, pueblo against pueblo. In historic times the Hopi town of Awatovi was destroyed by other Hopi for accepting Spanish missionaries. However, little archaeological evidence exists for internecine warfare. Proponents of this hypothesis rightly ask what kind of evidence would one expect; the hypothesis is not easily testable in an archaeological context because a different, potentially hostile culture would not be identifiable in the archaeological record.

Epidemic disease brought on by crowded, unsanitary conditions sometimes has been suggested as a contributing factor to Anasazi abandonment. A Spanish expedition to the Hopi villages in 1780 reported that the Hopis were suffering so greatly from hunger and "pestilence" that they were in the last stages of extermination. Excavators of cliff dwellings are often amazed at the quantity of human feces found in abandoned, garbage-filled rooms, in close proximity to dwelling rooms. The feces infested with parasitic, spiny-headed worms found on the floor of the Dot Klish phase pithouse testify to the potentially epidemic health problems faced by the Anasazi.

Few modern scholars who have examined the potential of disease as a cause for depopulation have pointed out that it is directly linked to malnutrition. It is not difficult to envision a deteriorating environment, failing crops, a deficient diet resulting in malnutrition, disease, a declining population, and eventual abandonment. However, disease is usually thought to play only an ancillary role in the depopulation of a region. After all, the Hopi have clung to their mesa-top villages despite devastating epidemics of Spanish-introduced diseases.

The most widely accepted abandonment theory focuses on environmental change. Geologic, tree-ring, and pollen studies indicate erosion, denuding of the land, and a decrease in rainfall around A.D. 1150. These factors conspired to make agriculture difficult or impossible in many areas that had been marginal even in better years.

It stands to reason that marginal areas, the ones that were last to be occupied as population grew and the climate became more amenable to agriculture, would be the first to be abandoned in hard times. A lowering of the mean monthly temperature by a few degrees or a drop of an inch or so in average summer rainfall might make a difference in the size of the food surplus in a good environmental setting for agriculture; in more marginal areas, it may have been the difference between staying or leaving, or even life and death.

In all likelihood a deteriorating environment was a major factor in the abandonment of northern Black Mesa, but overpopulation, disease, and other factors also may have played important roles. Most of the factors are natural rather than cultural, and yet the social element in large part determines the kinds of responses people have to environmentally or culturally induced stress. Determining the social responses to stress can be exceedingly difficult, for archaeologists are not equipped to be paleopsychologists. Yet it is important to know, for example, how social organization is affected by stress. Does clan affiliation, which encourages sharing, allow postponement of abandonment? What social options are available to the populations? Does the social organization encourage movement by nuclear families or much larger groupings? Is decision-making an individual or group process? These kinds of questions demonstrate that the concept of abandonment cannot be viewed simply as a movement of population.

Archaeological evidence from the end of the Toreva phase gives us some insight into the Black Mesa abandonment process. It can be assumed that the tremendous stress which caused the decision to move did not arise instantaneously, but rather increased over a period of several years, or even over a decade or so.

Several studies in other parts of the Southwest have shown that a threat to the prehistoric subsistence base produced an attempt at diversification. If the corn crop was a partial failure, attempts were made to gather more wild plants and hunt more animals. On Black Mesa, as the Toreva phase progressed, it appears there was greater experimentation and reliance on a more varied food supply.

At some point, however, the experimentation failed, and a decision was made to move. The move was not far, probably to the central and southern parts of Black Mesa and to the canyon country to the north. All portable objects were taken, even the very heavy manos and metates. Of the hundreds of Toreva phase mealing bins that were excavated, not more than one or two contained a metate. Only broken and worn out grinding tools were left behind. This may indicate a short move to a planned location, since manos and metates were made of the sandstone found all over Anasazi country.

It is interesting to contrast the Black Mesa abandonment with abandonment in other areas in the Southwest. In the White Mountains south of Black Mesa large sites were sometimes abandoned with virtually everything left in place, as if one day the women went to the fields and the men went hunting, but for some reason never returned. Hundreds of vessels were left behind. Flaking tools and partially finished projectile points are found on the dwelling floors. North of Black Mesa, sites are occasionally found where metates are lined up against the wall and then deliberately broken, perhaps indicating the migrants' inability to take large heavy tools and their wish that nobody else use them. These examples demonstrate different abandonment processes which, with detailed study, could provide new insights into Anasazi population movements; they also show that abandonment cannot be examined as an isolated phenomenon.

﷽ KLETHLA PHASE (EARLY PUEBLO III), A.D. 1150 to 1250

People of the Klethla phase and the following Tsegi phase did not live on northeastern Black Mesa; however, the cultural developments of earlier periods can be better understood in light of these descendants of Toreva phase people. This brief outline of these two phases is gleaned fron non-BMAP projects done north of the mesa and some random BMAP surveys done on the interior and southern parts of the mesa.

The Klethla phase is important because it saw the formation of new communities after major population shifts, and also because it was a period of great experimentation and culture change. In spite of the potential lodestone the Klethla phase represents for understanding Anasazi culture change, virtually no sites dating to this phase have been excavated.

This seems to be due to the fact that there are few Klethla phase cliff dwellings, so they escaped the diligent search for perishable materials in the early days of southwestern archaeology. Second, they represent a period of time when the ubiquitous Pueblo II sites disappeared and were replaced by much fewer, but larger communities in restricted geographical settings. This localization of settlement decreases the likelihood that Klethla phase sites will be disturbed by construction, and therefore the likelihood of funding for excavation. Nevertheless, some generalizations can be made based on a few partially excavated sites and from observations made during surface reconnaissance.

During the Klethla phase, which lasted from A.D. 1150 to 1250, settlements changed abruptly from small, localized, single-lineage settlements to larger, probably multilineage villages. This change is suggested not only by the increased size of the sites but by their configuration. Many Klethla phase communities have multiple kivas and are characterized by a square or rectangular shape of four lines of rooms enclosing a central plaza. Multiple kivas indicate separate kiva societies or lineages and probably represent the amalgamation of several smaller, displaced villages.

The occurrence of a large interior plaza or courtyard at a site often has been interpreted by archaeologists as evidence that there was village-wide or pan-village ceremonial participation. Plazas are used for these purposes in Pueblo communities today. While separate kivas hint at socially segmented villages and are perhaps a holdover from smaller, socially cohesive communities, the plaza represents the integration of a larger, more complex social unit.

As we know, a large community is not simply a magnified version of a smaller one. It exhibits qualitative as well as quantitative differences. Both social and economic functions are different. Some anthropologists have developed a mathematical yardstick for determining the relationship of population size to social complexity and while this has not been rigorously tested on a prehistoric population on a local level, the Anasazi might prove an apt test case.

This was an era of culture change and population movement throughout the entire Anasazi country. Generally, the upland areas were abandoned; Chaco culture became disorganized and Chaco Canyon itself was largely deserted. The stability that seemed to exist in the preceding centuries was shattered, resulting in large-scale migration and a restructuring of social institutions.

Not accidentally these changes are coincident with the occurrence of large-scale sheet erosion, arroyo cutting, and a general worsening of the environment. While it is difficult to generalize for the entire Colorado Plateau, the movement of people tended to be toward lower elevations and to areas with a more dependable water supply and a higher water table.

🌿 TSEGI PHASE (LATE PUEBLO III), A.D. 1250 to 1300

The brief Tsegi phase resulted in the construction of numerous cliff dwellings about twelve miles north of Black Mesa in what is now Navajo National Monument. Kiet Siel, Betatakin, and Inscription House are familiar names, and photographs of these sites set against striking red canyon walls have enhanced countless issues of *Arizona Highways* (Fig. 6.1).

Tsegi phase occupation was not restricted to these cliff dwellings, however. A few smaller ones are found on the south-central part of Black Mesa, and a number of large sites were constructed in the open. Because they are in less spectacular settings and have been ravaged by time and the elements, the open sites have not attracted as much attention. The grandiose cliff dwellings and the majestic settings bewitched early explorers and archaeologists, and consequently they have been the object of intensive exploration and exploitation since their discovery. In spite of this attention, only in the last fifteen years or so have the ruins been scientifically investigated. Most of this excellent work has been done in Tsegi Canyon by archaeologist-dendrochronologist Jeff Dean of the Tree-Ring Laboratory at the University of Arizona.

Tsegi Canyon was only sparsely occupied until A.D. 1250 because the deep, narrow gorge provided little in the way of farming potential. These narrow canyons, however, became the last resort of the Kayenta Anasazi as erosion and the dropping water table made previous habitation zones unsuitable for agriculture. While the amount of arable land in the valley bottoms was limited, most of the occupied caves of Tsegi Canyon were associated with incalculably valuable, reliable springs; water still flows in the bottom of the wash.

The major foci of Dean's study were the 135-room Betatakin and the 155-room Kiet Siel villages. His research attempted to determine how the villages were formed and grew, a process he could investigate because of the large number of tree-ring specimens obtainable from roof beams and support posts. Two hundred ninety-eight specimens were retrieved from Betatakin alone, making it the best dated prehistoric ruin in the world. By dating the

Figure 6.1. Kiet Siel, a Tsegi phase cliff dwelling north of Black Mesa

construction of individual rooms, he could determine the construction sequence of the cliff dwellings.

Dean isolated what he called room clusters. Each cluster is composed of a dwelling, one to six storage chambers (small granaries and storerooms), occasionally a corn mealing room, and a courtyard (open areas with a fire pit and mealing bins). The room cluster is the basic architectural and social unit of the Tsegi phase, each cluster probably housing an extended family.

While there was a small occupation of the Betatakin cave by A.D. 1250, the nucleus of the village was formed in 1267 when three large room clusters were built. A fourth was added in 1268, after which the village grew more slowly. It appears that the village was founded by a group that existed as a social unit elsewhere prior to the founding of Betatakin. This is suggested by the planned nature of the initial occupation and the fact that it was made up of a number of room clusters. The slow growth of the village after the initial occupation was probably a result of internal population growth and the marrying-in of spouses rather than immigration of new household groups. A total of about 125 people lived in the village at its peak in the mid-1280s, and abandonment occurred between 1286 and 1300.

The building sequence at Kiet Siel is in sharp contrast to that of Betatakin. Village growth seems to have been the result of separate migrations indicating that the people came from various sources rather than a single community as was the case at Betatakin. In some cases, the larger villages resulted from the amalgamation of populations from various sources; in other cases, the basic village was the result of a single community moving into Tsegi Canyon as one cohesive social unit and increasing through internal population growth.

By A.D. 1300, however, the deteriorating environment which had necessitated the move to the canyon country caught up with the Anasazi. The continuing erosion and cutting of arroyos into the alluvium of the canyon bottoms meant that while both water and soil were still available, these two crucial elements for farming could not be brought together. The cutting of the arroyos lowered the small streams below the level of the land. Without pumps or water wheels, the Anasazi had no means of getting the water to the farm plots. The only alternative was to move once again.

⟨ɤ⟩ PUEBLO IV, A.D. 1300 to 1600

This move, marking the end of the Tsegi phase and the beginning of Pueblo IV, proved more permanent, for the migration was to the peninsulas on the southern edge of Black Mesa, where eventually these people evolved into the modern Hopi.

During this period the artifacts and architecture become truly reflective of the historic Pueblos. Anasazi society seems to have become reoriented, perhaps in part as a result of the aggregation of population into ever larger communities. Small villages do not need the more formal social and economic organization that is required for towns and cities. Specializations of arts and crafts seem to have been partially a function of community size as was the specialization of religious and political positions. Trade between Pueblo areas increased. The ceramic tradition in some areas changed dramatically; the inspiration for the beautiful yellow pottery with dark brown and red decorations which was a precursor of Hopi ceramics may have come from Mexico. Rio Grande pueblos have many indications of contact with Mexican high cultures. Kivas were often decorated with strikingly handsome, multicolored murals depicting dances and ceremonies recognizable today.

Coronado entered the pueblo of Zuni in 1540, the date often given as the end of the Pueblo IV period and the beginning of the historic period. This early incursion, however, did not have much impact on Hopi culture. It was only in 1598 with the arrival of soldiers, missionaries, and settlers who were committed to a program of forced culture change that the long and arduous process of attempting to reshape Hopi society began. The Spanish, of course, were only partially successful.

At least a few centuries before the Spanish entrada, the Navajo and Apache arrived in force. These tribes found the Pueblo peoples vulnerable, for there was raiding as well as trade between the two cultures, and later between the nomadic peoples and the Spanish.

While the Navajo were in the northern Southwest prior to the sixteenth century, the first evidence we have of Navajo on northeastern Black Mesa is in the mid-1800s. It is safe to assume, however, that the region was sporadically occupied and often traversed earlier. The Navajo have remained on Black Mesa to this day, using it for permanent habitation, piñon nut and wood gathering, and now as a source of coal which they pick up at the mine for heating their homes. They live between the mined areas, some still herd sheep, but most work as laborers for the mine or for archaeologists.

The tale of Black Mesa is not solely a step-by-step discussion that chronicles culture changes in as fine detail as possible. A number of major themes run through the tale, which because of their centrality to the question of why culture changes, have been given special emphasis. We turn next to these problem spheres—population, environment, subsistence, and adaptation.

7
The Problem Spheres

A LL ARCHAEOLOGISTS are interested in change as a phenomenon to be investigated. Whatever scale we use to measure change, be it the year in the Julian calendar or stages such as the "Age of Plastic," the "Atomic Era," or "Pueblo II," we devise an arbitrary framework for discussing events and conditions and for making comparisons to examine change or the lack of it.

The scope with which individual archaeologists examine change varies greatly. Some archaeologists are interested in how hunting and gathering societies evolved into agricultural ones, others in why a specific group of people moved from one valley to another, and others in universal processes of change regardless of time and space. We shall limit ourselves here to an understanding of change on Black Mesa.

The Black Mesa Archaeological Project has focused on 1) population change, especially the steep growth in the eleventh century, 2) abandonment of northeastern Black Mesa between A.D. 1100 and 1150, and 3) changes in land use through time. These changes can be examined from many perspectives, but the one that seems to be most productive is an examination of the society's changing relationship to the natural environment. While we have advocated an integrated, systemic research program and tried to avoid the pure "cause and effect" or "prime mover" type of explanation for cultural change, individual studies on Black Mesa have taken points of view that emphasize the role of environmental change and population pressure. An examination of the evolution of our ideas about culture change provides a perspective on the changing nature of archaeological inquiry.

At the same time, it is interesting to note that the broad research questions we are posing are essentially the same as those proposed by archaeologists a half century ago. Now, however, we phrase our hypotheses in a more sophisticated way and test them with new techniques. We are closer to the answers, and the questions are now phrased in such a way that they are potentially more answerable. More important, certain scenarios have proved untenable and have been eliminated as explanations.

▓ THE POPULATION

Ever since Malthus promulgated his ideas, population and competition for critical resources have been considered major factors in human history. Population growth has been considered both evil, the cause of war and famine, and good, permitting and encouraging urbanism and the attendant traits of civilization. Demographic studies exploring broad evolutionary change, such as the shift from hunting and gathering to agriculture or the origin and downfall of civilization, have focused on population as a "prime mover." That is, population increase has often been seen as the trigger which causes major cultural evolutionary change. A more successful approach has been to consider population as an integral subsystem of the entire cultural and natural system, not as *the* causative factor that regulates the rest of the system.

The first step in determining the relationship of demography to culture change is to find out just what the population was. While numerous methods exist for estimating population size, they all fall into two general categories, relative and absolute. Relative population figures depend on a temporal distinction; that is, one period compared to another so that it is possible to make statements such as "there appears to be a 10 percent increase in population during the such-and-such phase." Absolute population figures, which do not depend on comparison, state actual numbers of individuals. While it might appear that absolute figures are preferable, in many, if not most instances, archaeologists are simply concerned with trends rather than actual numbers. Specific figures are usually more difficult to obtain, and they may project a precision that is largely illusory.

One method of estimating population is to excavate a cemetery and get a body count. This approach permits the determination of actual population figures, mortality rates, diseases, sex ratios, and so on, but it does have drawbacks. If the site was occupied a long time, and the length of that time is difficult to determine accurately, it may make the population count unreliable. Furthermore, another cemetery area may be undiscovered or custom may have required burying corpses away from the site. An example would be the huge pueblos in Chaco Canyon, where only a small fraction of burials has been recovered. The large cemetery areas that must exist have never been found. Not uncommonly certain segments of the population may have been treated in death quite differently than the rest of the individuals. Witness the refusal of some churches to bury suicides in consecrated ground.

The number of skeletons recovered by BMAP has made it impossible to attempt this direct population count method. So few have been recovered that we would have to assume that there were not enough individuals in each phase to produce a second generation.

Population estimates in various parts of the world have been derived indirectly from food consumption calculations and amounts of food refuse. For example, by knowing how much shellfish it takes to sustain an individual, and by determining the amount of shellfish remains at a site along with the length of occupation at that site, a very rough approximation of the population figure can be obtained. Some ingenious attempts at describing population change in the Southwest have depended on how cooking vessels and hearth size changed through time. The assumption is that if a family cooks food in a common vessel over a common fire, vessel and hearth size will increase as families become larger. This method provides some information about population trends but not actual population figures. Although several methods have been employed, the two used most extensively on Black Mesa for determining population involve counting rooms and measuring the amount of floor space.

The study of demography on Black Mesa provides one of the best examples of how BMAP has refined methods over the years and how gathering additional data ha; permitted new interpretation. The first population study for northern Black Mesa was a crude attempt to determine relative fluctuations in population from phase to phase by counting the number of sites recorded for each phase. While a number of problems are associated with this technique, it was the only one available to us given the data at hand. One major problem is that changes in site size through time can signal or mask huge variations in numbers of people. In addition, the number of special use sites such as hunting camps can vary from phase to phase, phases may be of unequal or unknown length, or populations may have been more mobile in one phase than another, thereby "producing" more sites. All these factors singly and in combination can create wildly inaccurate pictures of the demographic situation when population is viewed solely in terms of numbers of sites per phase.

After more excavated sites were available for study, more refined techniques could be used so that population estimates could be based not only on number of sites but number of actual dwellings.

A study was done by Al Swedlund, who was teaching physical anthropology at Prescott College, and a Prescott College undergraduate, Steve Sessions. Their basic assumption was that population growth on Black Mesa was not mainly a result of immigration from other areas, but rather was due to an increasing birth rate, a decreasing death rate, or both. This is not to suggest that Black Mesans lived in cultural isolation from the rest of the Kayenta Anasazi and that their gene pool was being undiluted; however, the homogeneity of the archaeology and the internal consistency of the evolutionary sequence indicate that the population expansion largely did result from internal growth. Swedlund and Sessions defined a household in each excavated site as a room with a well-defined hearth, which distinguished it from the storage rooms. Kivas were not included in the sample. By using the Hopis as an example and by employing biological maintenance principles (the optimum number of family members in a biologically viable household), they came up with an average household figure of 5.55 individuals. By counting the average number of habitation rooms per site, and multiplying by 5.55 individuals, they derived a population figure for each excavated site in each phase. They then extrapolated from the figures derived from excavation to sites recorded on survey, but not excavated. This was done by multiplying the population estimate for the excavated sites by the number of recorded sites for each phase. Their results indicate a jump in population corresponding with the increase in the number of sites per phase (Fig. 7.1).

The increase was calculated from the earliest to the latest phase at 0.86 percent per year, a figure not at all surprising for nonindustrial society with a subsistence agricultural economy. They concluded by suggesting that the population of northern Black Mesa increased until about A.D. 1100, due to improved agricultural techniques, increasing dependence on agriculture, and an increasing ability to exploit the environment. By A.D. 1100, however, the population had overshot the carrying capacity of the land and the available technology. The environment could no longer support the population, and northern Black Mesa was abandoned.

Swedlund and Sessions are the first to acknowledge that their study provides only a rough approximation of the population, based on a number of somewhat shaky assumptions. The early surveys on which they based their work were imprecise in the measurement of site size. The assumption of a constant 5.55 individuals per household through time may be incorrect. Also erroneous may be the assumption that all sites in each phase were occupied for the length of that phase, while in reality some sites may be the result of the same people moving to different locations during the same phase. This error would create the impression of a much larger population on Black Mesa than actually existed.

An interesting aspect of their work, however, is that while they derived actual population figures for each phase, the numbers are useful only as a measurement of percentage change from phase to phase, and are not meant to be a real index of number of individuals. Their method refined a relative population technique, almost a hybrid of relative and absolute.

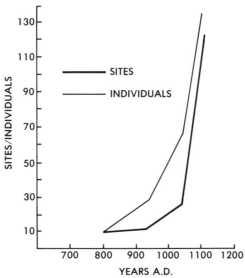

Figure 7.1. Changes in the number of sites and individuals through time, as determined by Swedlund and Sessions

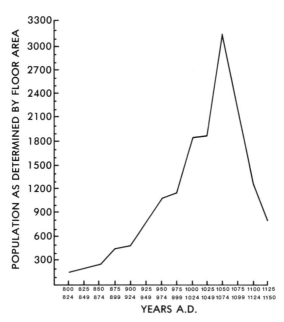

Figure 7.2. Population changes on Black Mesa, as determined by Layhe

The study had its desired effect. It proved its heuristic value by getting other students interested in the population problem of Black Mesa, especially an SIU graduate student named Bob Layhe, who wrote his master's thesis on the topic. With the results of the intensive survey of the eastern lease area to use as an additional data base, Layhe expanded on the earlier study. Instead of number of sites or number of habitation rooms, he used as one measure the amount of actual living space at a site. Not unreasonably, he assumed that in a simple egalitarian farming society, there is a relationship between the size of a family and the amount of space it uses—no grandiose swinging bachelor penthouses on Black Mesa! Second, Layhe assumed that as a community's population increased, so would its size—again, not an earth-shaking premise. His final assumption was that the larger the population, the greater the number of artifacts to be found. Using statistical techniques, he worked from the known (the excavated sites) to the unknown (the surveyed sites), estimating for surveyed sites the floor area of rooms based on site size and the density of artifacts. By using a more refined chronology than was available to the earlier investigators, he was able to place the sites within 25-year periods, from A.D. 800 to 1150. The estimated floor area for each site was then plotted against the time scale of 25-year increments to produce the population curve (Fig. 7.2).

Immediately one can see greater variation than in the earlier curve. This is to be expected, given that the chronology is divided into smaller units, and it is a more realistic view of human population dynamics. The most glaring discrepancy between the two curves is the period at which the peak population occurs. While the Swedlund and Sessions model shows a steady population increase until the time of abandonment, Layhe's model indicates that population peaked from the period of about A.D. 1050 to 1074.

The discrepancies between the two curves might be due to differences in how the archaeologists collected and analyzed their data, or they might be due to the real situation—always difficult to detect. It seems, in this case, that it is a bit of both. The more precise temporal measurement, the more quantifiable survey data, indicate that Layhe's population curve may better represent reality. On the other hand, the population curves were drawn from data in different areas, Swedlund and Session's from the western lease area and Layhe's from the eastern lease area. While these two areas are very close and, in fact, contiguous for the most part, their environments are different. The eastern area is higher, cooler, wetter and more rugged, with narrower washes. Before abandoning the area, people may have been moving from the eastern to the western area. This scenario would mean a much more constant population for the late periods on northern Black Mesa as a whole, with shifts in population occurring within the range of only a few miles.

Bob Layhe is finding fault with his data and procedures and is refining the population curve as part of his doctoral dissertation. While population change should not be viewed as the deus ex machina for the explanation of culture change, neither can it be ignored. Population affects the environment as well as being affected by it, and, in fact, is a component of the environment. It is a crucial aspect of the cultural system any archaeologist investigates, and any attempt to clarify prehistoric demography must be applauded.

The interesting archaeological lesson the study of Black Mesa demography provides is the continual and necessary refining of the population curve by an increase of our data base over the years, improved methods of observing and recording data, and more sophisticated methods of analysis of those data.

More can be determined about the population by directly examining human skeletons and how they were interred. A major disappointment of BMAP has been the inability to recover more burials, not only because they provide important direct information about demography but also because they supply information about social status, nutrition, and pathologies.

Obviously, the accoutrements found with the body of King Tutankhamun indicated he was not an ordinary Egyptian farmer or pyramid construction hand. Exceptions to the rule of more and better grave goods meaning higher status are not uncommon, however. When King Faisal of Saudi Arabia was assassinated in 1975, he was the leader of his government and one of the wealthiest men in the world. Yet he was interred in a simple shroud in a plot encircled by stones, undistinguishable from the bodies of commoners in the same cemetery.

Figure 7.3. Debbie Martin catalogs skeletal remains from a late Black Mesa site.

Nevertheless, style of burial can be important in determining status. Patterns of skeletal and tooth growth as well as pathologies are important indicators of nutritional health.

Debbie Martin, one of Al Swedlund's graduate students at the University of Massachusetts, and John Ravesloot of SIU decided to examine 70 individuals from Black Mesa to derive status and nutritional information and the relationship between them. Because of the small sample and the preliminary state of their studies, their conclusions are tentative but very tantalizing (Fig. 7.3).

The 70 burials consisted of 32 adults (20 males and 12 females) and 38 infants and juveniles. Most were buried in earthen grave pits which were excavated through trash heaps. In one instance the incomplete remains of a fetus of four to five months was found placed on a large potsherd and deposited in a shallow grave scooped out of the trash deposit. In some instances there was additional preparation of the grave pit. Some burials were covered with sandstone slabs, others had slab-lined pits, and one was in a slab-lined pit with a log covering. All the burials that were treated in this special way had grave goods, usually vessels, presumably containing food, and in most cases in larger numbers than those found in common earthen pits. No children were found in specially prepared graves, suggesting that this type of burial was restricted to adults. Adults, however, were also found in simple earthen pits, perhaps indicating that more elaborate burials were restricted to adults who had attained some special status in life. This is not to suggest that there were major class differences on Black Mesa, but rather that due to age, sex, or accomplishments, some individuals had greater prestige than others, and this was reflected in how they were buried.

The interpretation of high and low status individuals was enhanced by nutritional studies. The assumption was made that higher status individuals would be in a better nutritional state because of better access to food. Preliminary studies did indeed show differences in diet-related stress between individuals in high and low status burials, between males and females, and between adults and children.

Various sophisticated nutrition studies were performed, even involving teeth. It is possible to determine dietary stress by observing incidences of thinness of tooth enamel when the tooth is cut and viewed in cross section, almost as periods of stress are indicated in trees by very narrow rings. The distance of the enamel disturbance from the tooth edge gives an indication of the age at which the stress occurred. Eighty-two percent of the individuals showed evidence of dietary stress in tooth enamel with the greatest period of trauma between the ages of two and six.

All of the skulls examined had mild to severe forms of what is called porotic hyperostosis and cribra orbitalia, which is a pitting and reforming of the bone along the top, sides, and upper walls of the eye orbits. Instead of normal bone growth there is a spongy, thin-walled growth. These pathologies are associated with severe iron deficiency anemia, and while adult males have healed or mild forms of the disease, the severest cases are found in females and children. Osteoporosis is a thinning and a sponginess of bone resulting from old age or a dietary deficiency. This condition was common in young adult females but not in adult males.

Finally, long bones were x-rayed for lines which indicate periods of absence of growth as a result of a nutrition deficiency. Growth arrest lines were consistently found in the female but not the male population.

The combination of burial practices and nutritional evidence points to the fascinating relationship between culture and environment. Adult males have fewer and milder cases of multiple pathologies and furthermore those in more elaborate graves were even more healthy than the norm, having 33 percent fewer pathologies. Females on the other hand, have a higher incidence of nutritional stress which in part may be related to childbearing and lactation during the reproductive years, but which may also be a result of their lower status and consequently lesser access to food. How many of us can remember our mothers giving our fathers the center cut and the second helping? Furthermore, adult males probably had greater access to protein because of their involvement with hunting parties. The most consistently stressed individuals, however, were children. Every child shows more than one type of growth stress from dietary deficiency. The difference between sexes is that, if they lived, the males were able to overcome the disabilities, while the effects on the females were more severe and continued into adulthood.

So much for the noble savage, living an egalitarian existence and being in good health from eating nothing but natural foods. Times were tough.

❧ ENVIRONMENT

Environment must be fairly well understood if any archaeologist is going to use a cultural ecological approach for understanding adaptational change. In the arid Southwest modern farmers find mother nature capricious and economic existence precarious. Like them, prehistoric farmers were directly dependent on temperature and rainfall.

Care must be taken, however, to ensure that environment and its interrelationship with culture is kept in a proper perspective and not viewed as a prime mover. To suggest a one-to-one correlation between environmental change and culture change is to fall prey to all the dangers of the environmental determinism of the last century which overemphasized and oversimplified the role of environment in culture change.

While nonindustrial societies tend to interact directly with their environment, the relationship between environment and human behavior is varied and multifaceted, for culture can respond in any manner of ways to similar environments. In short, while everybody talks about the weather, there *is* something they can do about it! Unquestionably, environmental changes of certain magnitudes require some adaptive changes in behavior. The nature of the human response is determined largely by cultural variables such as the nature and security of the subsistence base, social networks, and settlement patterns, among others. Any understanding of the interaction of culture and environment, therefore, demands detailed knowledge of both. Furthermore, the simple concordance of environmental change and cultural change does not necessarily mean that a changing environment caused adaptational shifts. The causes of culture change are almost limitless. There are some instances where culture change in simple societies caused environmental change which was reflected in the archaeological record. The difficult task then, for the archaeologist who perceives the co-occurrence of environmental and cultural change, is to determine the nature of that relationship.

The driving force behind these studies is Dr. Thor N.V. Karlstrom, a geologist for the U.S. Geological Survey (U.S.G.S) in Flagstaff, whose passion is the reconstruction of past environments. By bringing individuals such as Karlstrom to BMAP, we ensured the multidisciplinary nature of the project, which was essential if we were to use the cultural ecological approach for understanding human behavior.

As has been stated, modern archaeology demands the cooperation of many types of scientists. Unfortunately, archaeologists too often have found this cooperation lacking largely as a result of their own actions. We hope to attract to our projects the best botanists, geologists, and others. They are usually professionals who have gone through training every bit as rigorous as our own, which means that they are intelligent individuals anxious to do research—research of their own design. Too often the archaeologists who need the talents of these scientists treat them as ancillary personnel whose task is to identify, do minimal interpretation, and leave the broad synthesis to the archaeologist. Naturally, these "ancillary" scientists become disenchanted and go off to pursue their own research interests.

During the course of BMAP we learned that we should not expect a complete overlap of research interests. What we did was encourage and partially support competent scientists who have *some* interest in our problems, to become involved with the project. Where interest, need, and data overlap, we cooperated. Where research interests diverge, we encourged them to pursue their own work. To do otherwise would drive the most competent individuals from cooperative research.

Karlstrom encouraged this approach among the archaeologists and other scientists. He also underscored the crucial confirming effect of independent lines of evidence as a basic research tool. If, for example, the zoologist, tree-ring specialist, and geologist all have reasonably good indications of a climate change at a particular time, that evidence is very strong, perhaps even constituting proof, since each line of evidence is independent of the other.

This kind of working relationship was developed in the summer of 1965, when I was at the Museum of Northern Arizona and Karlstrom, through the U.S.G.S., hired me to date some recent geology by identifying partially buried sites in the Hopi Buttes area south of Black Mesa. That work eventually became my dissertation and established the symbiotic relationship that exists between us to this day.

To reconstruct the past Black Mesa environment we relied mainly on the results of geological, tree-ring, and plant pollen studies. The evidence for past culture change comes, of course, from archaeology, the results of which have already been reported.

Analysis of paleoclimate by tree-ring analysis is easily understood in principle. A growing season which tends to be favorable to corn, beans, and squash should also be advantageous for tree growth, producing a wide annual ring. Studies have shown that southwestern tree growth is highly correlated with climate, especially precipitation. By constructing several series, or index, chronologies for a region it is possible to develop an annual climate chart going back to the time of Christ, since not only does the ring reflect climate, but it can be dated to a single year.

To construct the index chronology, each annual ring measurement is converted to a standardized index using a procedure which emphasizes climate-related variables. Nonclimatically related variables, such as the fact that more recently formed rings on a tree tend to be narrower, are factored out. Each annual index from individual trees in a specific region is averaged to produce a composite tree ring index for the area. It is then possible to determine the years of average rainfall and measure wetter and drier variations from the norm. Because the dating accuracy of dendrochronology is to within a single year, most climatic chronologies based on tree rings are averaged on a 10- or 25-year basis. To attempt to correlate yearly climate change with an archaeological phase would be very difficult because of the relative inaccuracy of phase dates and the fact that the annual tree-ring chronology would produce too much information, making it difficult to establish climatic trends (Fig. 7.4).

Figure 7.4. Workers soak charred beams in gasoline and wax, then wrap them with string to protect them for shipment to the Laboratory of Tree-Ring Research at the University of Arizona for dating.

Data from plant pollen are more difficult to interpret in terms of paleoenvironmental reconstruction. Amazingly enough, the seemingly delicate, usually yellow pollen that sticks to your fingers when you touch the stamens of flowers is almost indestructible if buried. Palynologists, specialists in plant pollen, often work with microscopic bits of plant many thousands of years old. Pollen is important not only because it resists the depredations of time, but because the pollen of many species of plants has a highly distinctive shape, permitting ready identification. And, of course, different species of plants reflect different environments.

Since pollen is present almost everywhere, as any hay fever sufferer can attest, and it does not need to be charred to enhance preservation, a series of pollen samples taken from an arroyo or trench can provide evidence for climatic change. If, for example, soil samples taken every 10 centimeters apart in the face of an arroyo show a gradual increase in the ratio of pine pollen to weed pollen as the samples get closer to the surface, a gradual decrease in temperature and an increase in moisture can be assumed. If the investigator is fortunate enough to be able to date the stratum by geological cross reference to other deposits or by radiocarbon from wood in the same geologic stratum, then absolute dates can be affixed to certain climate regimes. In this way pollen can be used in a noncultural context for reconstructing past environmental fluctuations.

The methods of pollen analysis are simple. The palynologist extracts the pollen from soil samples taken from a recently exposed surface and seals it immediately in a plastic bag so modern pollen rain does not contaminate the sample and bias the interpretation. The soil is dissolved from the pollen by strong acids which do not harm the pollen. After being preserved in silicone oil and mounted on slides, pollen grains are examined under a microscope and species are counted.

Relative ratios of pollen from different plant species, however, do not signify a one-to-one correspondence to the plants themselves. Pollen of some wind-pollinated plants such as pine may be dispersed over great areas and others, like corn, may be found only near the base of the plant. As a result, pine may seem to be more widespread than it is, and corn is underrepresented in the record. Some plants are prolific producers of pollen and others are not. The clearing of trees for farm land and the human activity around a village can destroy some plant species and encourage others, presenting a distorted view of the climate. Furthermore, the pollen of some plant species preserves better than others. All these factors can distort the climatic interpretation. Palynologists use complex formulae they have derived to try to take these factors into account; however, there is disagreement as to the efficacy of these efforts.

Recent geology, and the hydrologic factors it represents, are also difficult to interpret but can add a great deal of confirming evidence when coupled with studies of other disciplines.

The model used on Black Mesa, and confirmed by tree-ring and pollen evidence, suggests that during periods when the land surface is building due to water-deposited materials, the climate is wetter and the water table is rising. During periods when deposition is not occurring, the climate is drier and there is a lower regional water table. Arroyo cutting, or the deep entrenchment of washes due to erosion, seems to begin during transitional periods between major wet and dry climatic regimes or during a lowering of the water table. Minor interruptions in depositional units indicating a lessening of the generally wetter period are distinguished by levels showing the beginnings of soil development, buried root zones, and buried archaeological material.

To record the geological stratigraphy in the detail necessary to establish the depositional sequence, Karlstrom and his U.S.G.S. colleagues traveled thousands of miles on and around Black Mesa, measuring the different stratigraphic levels in hundreds of major and minor arroyos. They were especially alert for any stratigraphic units that contained organic material, such as twigs, pine cones, or forest litter, that could be used for radiocarbon-dating the various layers. It is only possible, as in the case of environmental reconstruction by pollen, to tie the regional geologic sequence into the tree-ring sequence by dating the deposits within a certain level of confidence.

An especially fortunate occurrence was Karlstrom's discovery of what we somewhat grandiosely called a buried forest in the heart of Black Mesa, south of the coal lease area. This low, quarter-mile-wide, mile-long valley was filled with juniper trees which had been killed by sand and clays that had washed into the valley so rapidly that the trees, while buried, remained standing, often with small twigs still on the branches. These trees could be seen

Figure 7.5. A juniper tree, part of the "buried forest," killed by rapid deposition of soil. The tree is being exposed by erosion.

because after they were buried and had died, an arroyo cut through the center of the valley, reexposing many of them in profile (Fig. 7.5). Once the buried trees were discovered in the walls of the arroyo, we were alerted to many buried trees by branch tips poking up around the valley. Discovered close to the sides of the valley were young, living, juniper trees which were being buried while one hundred yards away in the center of the valley, previously buried and killed trees were being exposed by erosion. In one miniscule valley, textbook examples of the dramatic processes of deposition and erosion were present at the same time.

Geology and hydrology were not the only attractions of what we have come to call Dead Juniper Wash. What brought our attention to the valley in the first place were several ruins with walls still standing some 10 feet high. These sites, while small, were clustered on the low sandstone ridges that form the edge of the valley. They date to the Klethla or Tsegi phase and represent the later occupation of Black Mesa some distance from the higher northeastern region.

Dead Juniper Wash was a potential key to environmental interpretation because of the easily observable geologic strata in the arroyo, the abundance of buried trees for dating, potential datable buried sites, and the late sites on the valley's edge.

With these facts in mind, this tiny topographic feature became the object of a major campaign. For four days Karlstrom and a second geologist, Jeff Dean (a tree-ring specialist), and his colleague, Dick Hevly (a palynologist), Bob Euler, myself, and a group of students camped in that slight dip in the middle of Black Mesa. We measured and counted, mapped and charted, collected and compared what natural and cultural evidence we could detect. I am sure the evening discussions around the campfire will be etched forever in the memories of everyone in that party, for it was then that we really started communicating in the lingua franca of multidisciplinary research.

The archaeology was somewhat disappointing. Few datable buried sherds were found, and the high-walled late sites at the valley's edge contained few artifacts. Nevertheless, the environmental data provided a major part of the framework for our investigations into the relationship between climate and cultural change. Eventually, buried trees were discovered in other areas, so that along with other paleoenvironmental and cultural data, we were able to propose a model of population and climate change for most of the Anasazi area.

The buried trees were important, not only because they were datable and demonstrated the rapidity with which deposition and erosion occurred, but because these geologic and hydrologic processes were taking place in the present and provided a model for what happened in the past. The trees did not germinate and die by burial at random time intervals, but rather in certain specific clusters of years. By determining the best conditions for tree germination, another major block of data was brought to bear on the regional paleoenvironmental interpretation.

A great amount of complex data from many different sources is focused on the paleoenvironmental question. What the figures demonstrate is a strong coincidence between environment and culture change, but they cannot provide us with the understanding of the complex interaction of the Black Mesa population and the natural environment. That kind of interpretation and explanation requires a combination of social theory about human behavior in nonindustrial societies in response to environmental change and the facts of environmental change determined by work such as that of Karlstrom and his colleagues.

◥ SUBSISTENCE

One of the major observable changes in the course of human existence has been our increasing ability to harness various forms of energy. In fact, these changes are often so readily apparent and dramatic that they have been used in many schemes as indicators of change and as stage names—witness the "age of electricity," the "industrial revolution," and "the atomic age." On Black Mesa we are, of course, dealing with a relatively short time span during which the quantity of energy produced and consumed did not change dramatically. We are studying a preindustrial agricultural society, and the changes in energy production and consumption focus largely on the collection or production of food.

Anthropologists always have been acutely aware of the cultural evolutionary significance of the shift from societies dependent on hunting and gathering to those dependent on grown foods. The domestication of plants and animals, although not a rapid process, was one of the crucial developments in human history. As far as we know, all prehistoric remains found on northern Black Mesa are those of agriculturalists, but no society is totally dependent on grown foods. We find charred kernels of domesticated corn as well as wild seeds and the bones of butchered animals in sites from all periods on Black Mesa. It is the change in ratio of these food types that helps us understand change in major behavioral systems.

To reconstruct a prehistoric subsistence system the archaeologist must reconstruct the past environment. He must understand in some detail the technological capabilities of the people who exploited that environment. He must determine what plants or animals were available, what could have been raised, and the nature of these organisms.

A detailed environmental analysis enables the archaeologist to estimate how many people the region could sustain. The carrying capacity is not a fixed figure but varies as the environment, population, and technology change. Most archaeology projects use a two-pronged approach to reconstructing ancient subsistence systems. The remains of the foods and the tools used for collecting and processing them are acquired through excavation, and hints at past food availability are obtained from study of the contemporary environment.

Usually, the most obvious indication of a food source in the Black Mesa excavation was animal bones. In attempting to reconstruct past diet, however, these bones provide little intellectual nourishment. There are numerous chances for error in attempting to determine diet from animal remains, errors can be made on many levels, and they tend to be cumulative and to compound one another (Fig. 7.6). A detailed examination of the methods involved in this process will underscore the complex and tedious nature of environmental and dietary reconstruction.

Archaeologists, or more often biologists as part of an archaeological team, use the contemporary animal population as a guide to what may have been available to the prehistoric population. This is done by consulting publications about faunal distribution, by trapping and observing in the study area, or both. Obviously the filter of time is involved, for the archaeological record will produce animal species not currently found in the study area, and vice versa.

The next source of bias is the genetic and morphological makeup of the animals. For example, rabbits are smaller than deer, but they are much more plentiful. Thus, in terms of availability, small rabbits may be more important to the prehistoric diet than large deer. Also bones of different animal species are variously preserved. The small, delicate bones of birds or mice do not have the density of a bear haunch and, as a result, may preserve differently, skewing the record.

Another characteristic of animal species affecting their representation in human diet is their social habits and behavior while being pursued. A biologist turned archaeologist, Kent Flannery, has pointed out that antelope and jackrabbits were most successfully hunted by groups of people using drives and other herding techniques. Antelope are social animals that congregate in bands,

Figure 7.6. Steps that are necessary to reconstruct a prehistoric diet from animal bones and the various biases that can occur in interpretation

and jackrabbits do not dig burrows but depend upon speed to escape. Deer and cottontails, on the other hand, are less social and more effectively hunted by individuals. The implication is that human societies organized in different ways can most effectively exploit different animal species.

The attempt at dietary reconstruction is made more difficult by the preferences of the hunter and the cook. Food preferences are one of the most culturally determined aspects of most societies. People have starved to death because they considered certain perfectly nutritious foods inedible. No group of people will eat the entire range of foods available to them. Certain foods may be taboo, for example those associated with clan names. The opposite may be the case, for certain foods have prestige value. If the price of caviar dropped to 85 cents a pound, few people would probably choose to eat it. Some animal species may, therefore, be overrepresented in the faunal collection due to undetectable cultural factors.

Butchering techniques affect species representation at sites. A hunter is less likely to lug home the entire carcass of a large animal; instead, he will butcher and perhaps eat some of the meat at the kill site. This indeed appears to be the case on Black Mesa where deer and antelope are represented mostly by foot bones and a few limbs, pelvic, and scapula bones. Never have more than 20 percent of the various skeletal elements from an individual been represented in excavation. By comparison, rabbits tend to have about 50 percent or more of their elements present. Few carnivore bones are found on Black Mesa, and when present they are usually limb or foot bones. This fits with the evidence from the historic Hopi and Navajo who hunt carnivores for their skins and only return with limb and foot bones attached to the hide.

The result then of this differential butchering is that it tends to overemphasize the importance of rabbits and downplay the deer and antelope in the diet.

Finally, disposal patterns may play a part in species representation at a site. There may be culturally determined patterns of disposal, large bones in one place, small in another, like the paper separated from the tin cans for the Tuesday morning garbage pickup. While the data from Black Mesa are inconclusive, other regions show variation of animal bone frequencies within the site.

The next set of potential biases are those that occur after disposal of the bones or after abandonment of the site. A major cause of destruction after bone disposal must have been domestic dogs and wild animals. Studies of Eskimo and Navajo disposal of animal remains show considerable destruction of bones after they are discarded. The domesticated dogs that we know were present on Black Mesa were not fed their daily ration of Alpo, but had to scavenge for their meals. Numerous bones from the excavations, including those of humans from burials, show evidence of gnawing. There is the possibility that larger bones were preferred by the carnivores which would mean overrepresentation of rodent and rabbit bones.

Another source of bias is the difficulty in distinguishing one animal species from another or, in the case of bones made into tools, the identifying characteristics may be removed in the

Figure 7.7. Identifying animal bones recovered from excavation to attempt to reconstruct the diet of Black Mesans

manufacturing process. Some individuals may be too young or too old to identify accurately, and some bones are too much like bones of another species to identify accurately. For example, a lumbar vertebra usually can be identified as belonging to a hooved animal but not as a deer, pronghorn, or mountain sheep.

The bones are identified on the basis of a comparative collection usually kept in a comparative osteology laboratory similar to a reference library (Fig. 7.7). Biologists who specialize in bone identification spend much time and effort collecting intact animals of known species and rendering the skin and flesh, labeling all the individual bones to be used to identify bones of unknown types found in excavations.

In many reports, interpretations about relative importance of individual species in the diet are based on the ratios of number of bones per species. There are several problems with this technique. Most bones are fragmentary, and it is often difficult or impossible to tell if two, ten, or twenty fragments are from the same bone element. It is the same class of problem as comparing numbers of potsherds if one type of vessel was broken into two pieces and the other type into a hundred. The second type would be unrealistically overrepresented in the counts. A second problem with this method is that different species have different numbers of bones. If the count is 100 pig foot bones and 100 sheep foot bones, the ratio is not one to one since pigs have 52 foot bones and sheep only 24.

Because of these problems on Black Mesa, we calculate the minimum number of individuals (MNI) for each species. This is accomplished by counting the largest number of elements, say a front leg bone from one side of an animal. Therefore, if the left and right front legs of a cottontail rabbit were found in a pithouse, they would be counted as the remains of one individual unless there was obvious difference in age or size. If there were fifteen front leg bones of a rabbit and nine are left (two of which are from immature rabbits) and six are right (three immature), ten is the MNI for rabbits, three of which are immature.

To calculate the economic importance of the various types of animal food, it is necessary to translate the MNI of each species into edible meat weights. The relative dietary importance of animals is not readily apparent from MNI, since smaller animals such as rabbits, which are often abundant, contribute far less meat to the table than do the rare but larger deer. The estimation of edible meat per animal species is a relatively crude figure because it is based on the *average* amount of meat per individual for any given species, and on the assumption that the weight of the bone and muscle and the edible meat weight are proportional.

As an indication of how site estimates of edible meat can vary, two widely used techniques were tested on the same data from an excavated site on Black Mesa. One method was to simply multiply the edible meat per individual animal by the MNI. The other method was to divide the edible meat weight of the individual animal by the weight of the skeleton multiplied by the weight of the skeleton multiplied by the weight of the bone excavated. The first method assumes all portions of an animal that are represented at all in the collection were eaten. The second method assumes that only those portions of meat represented by bones at the site were consumed. The different figures for determining edible meat for the same site were 1) using MNI—257,063 grams and 2) using figures derived from the weight of bones found—775.6 grams. Furthermore, rabbit made up 2.8 percent of the total edible meat at the site according to Method 1, while for Method 2 the figure was 7.9 percent. Because of the various cultural and natural forces that affect the presence, absence, and amount of bone that is recovered at a site by archaeologists, we have used the MNI to estimate edible meat represented at a site.

This detailed chronicle of the dependence of archaeologists on assumptions built upon assumptions gives one pause when statements are made such as "there was a slight shift in dependence on antelope (52 percent of the meat diet) to rabbit (18 percent of the meat diet) from phase X to Y." The statements become even more problematical when data on animal statistics are used to help interpret, confirm, or deny statements about human population trends or dependence on plant food.

Attempts to reconstruct the quantity of available food plants and the actual type and amount of the plant foods in the diet are hampered by the same problems as the reconstruction of meat availability and diet. Determination of the present plant community is, however, generally much easier; plants don't move, and the ones on Black Mesa at least are not nocturnal! Several studies were undertaken to provide the baseline measure of plant communities and their relationship to the underlying soil conditions on Black Mesa. These studies were done by measuring species density in predetermined and consistent sample blocks of land over the northeastern part of the mesa. The relative scarcity and abundance of the different species could be determined and compared to different localities.

On Black Mesa, floral analysis has received greater attention than bone studies because it provides a greater amount of usable data for the amount of time spent. Domestication of corn, beans, and squash on Black Mesa permitted population increase, permanence of settlement, and what little cultural elaboration there was. The ratio of that trinity of domesticated plants to wild plants and animals in the diet determined boom, bust, and all the stages in between. While the turkey and dog were domesticated and undoubtedly were eaten occasionally, there is no evidence that they were a major source of food.

A second reason for the emphasis on plant remains is that, for the Black Mesa region, vegetation is a more accurate indicator of total environment than is the animal population. All plants and animals exist within certain environmental parameters; however, some are more sensitive to shifts in their immediate environments than others. The ratio of plant species to one another helps us reconstruct the climate.

Figure 7.8. Seeds, roots, and charcoal bits are skimmed off soil samples as part of the process of reconstructing past vegetation and plant foods.

Past vegetation and plant utilization can be examined two ways. The most obvious is through the remains of the plants themselves in an archaeological context. Seeds, bits of leaves, squash rind, and the impression of plants in clay are all common finds. The other method, involving identification of plant pollen, is more subtle.

Archaeologists collect the larger plant remains in quite a different manner than they do pollen. A 1-liter soil sample is

Figure 7.9. Plant remains being sorted in the ethnobotany lab at the BMAP camp

taken from the northwest corner of every test square level at each site on Black Mesa. By knowing the exact amount of dirt removed from a site, it is possible to make quantitative statements such as, "In a comparison of 40 liters of earth from each period, the percentage of pumpkin seed increased 15 percent from Basketmaker III to Pueblo I." These soil samples are then taken back to camp where they are processed by flotation (Fig. 7.8). With the naked eye it is almost impossible to detect charred seeds and plant parts in the surrounding soil, and the parts are too small to be caught by the screen mesh. To separate the material, the soil samples are placed in a large tub of water, the heavy soil sinks to the bottom and the lighter seeds, charcoal bits, modern roots and other plant debris and sometimes small animal bones float or sink more slowly. The material is then skimmed off in a strainer and placed on newspaper to dry, carefully labeled as to the location of the site from which it came. Unfortunately, the dried and usually charred plant remains on the newspaper look to the naked eye like an indistinguishable mess. It is necessary to tease the organic material apart under a low-power microscope (Fig. 7.9). Modern intrusive seeds, rootlets, mouse droppings, and insect pupae are separated from

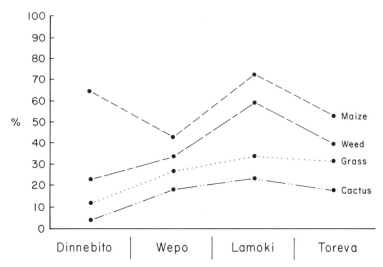

Figure 7.10. The percentages of maize, weed, grass, and cactus recovered from flotation samples by period in the Black Mesa sequence

what appears to be the archaeological context. The plant material is then identified and counted. Some identification is routine and other plant parts must be checked against a comparative collection, just as bones are identified with a reference collection (Fig. 7.10).

Pollen also can be used to infer plant diet. On Black Mesa we are only beginning to use pollen analysis on a large scale for this purpose. Plant pollen found in rooms can help determine their storage function. Pollen of domesticates can prove the cultivation of individual species and their relative frequency in the diet.

Certain cultural practices, however, can muddy the picture when pollen is used to determine the percentage of individual plant species in the diet. For example, corn pollen is used by the Pueblo Indians today, and was undoubtedly used by the Anasazi in ceremonies. The pollen is scattered on floors, altars, and other special areas, thereby overrepresenting corn in the total domesticate pollen picture.

In spite of the problems archaeologists and biologists encounter in determining diet and climate, plant and animal remains are the most effective means we have of reconstructing past subsistence systems. It is essential, however, that the limitations of the reconstruction be kept in mind and that continuing attempts be made to refine interpretations derived from floral and faunal analysis.

8

The Cultural Connection

IN THE LAST DECADE southwestern archaeology has consisted largely of a plethora of "little" studies, such as the relationship of the angle of slope on the ground surface to the distribution of surface artifacts or the ratio of bowls to jars in hunting camps. Nothing is inherently wrong with small-scale research questions—many have been described earlier in this volume—unless they are done as an end in themselves, as cute intellectual gimmicks, which do not contribute to a broader understanding of human behavior. Too often of late, the pieces of the large puzzle have been viewed as the puzzle itself.

Perhaps the trend to testing more narrowly focused hypotheses is a result of the deluge of raw data which has made it impossible for a single archaeologist, even with the aid of computers, to control all the information that impinges on a broadly cast question. It is certainly much easier to study the implications of the switch from one-hand to two-hand manos than to focus on the interrelationship between social organization, population change, and environmental change.

Another reason for the narrowness of many research efforts is the short-term, small-scale nature of many contract archaeology projects. Surveying and excavating along a 10-mile-long by 50-foot-wide sewer line right-of-way not only precludes an examination of "the big picture," but often hampers any attempts at a research orientation.

The preceding chapter dealing with problem spheres demonstrates how the narrowly focused small studies have been integrated and combined to solve problems much larger in scale, and in fact, how they have been necessary to answering questions about "the big picture." The size of cooking pots, houses, and communities, as well as dating techniques, interpretation of site function, and climatic indicators of various sorts have all been used to help determine and explain fluctuations in population size. Many small studies have to be undertaken and seemingly minor questions answered if we hope to solve the larger questions which prove so interesting.

As has been obvious throughout this narrative, the building-block studies involve many scholars and many disciplines. Not only are archaeologists uniquely dependent on a wide range of other social and natural scientists, but they must have more than a passing acquaintance with the method and theory and strengths and weaknesses of these other fields. The archaeologist must be able to evaluate the nonarchaeological as well as archaeological research in order to combine them into a holistic study elucidating the processes of human behavior. The integration of the many individual studies is the ultimate goal and the most difficult task—not only intellectually but logistically.

Often the specialized analyses are not done in a timely fashion, or they are done in a format not compatible with the larger study. Graduate students working on a specific problem flunk out or go to a different university. Theses that the archaeologist depends on are never completed and have to be assigned to other individuals. Many a final report has been held up for years and sometimes never published because a key piece of the research puzzle was not completed.

But what does completed really mean? In some instances, unfortunately, it is a simple descriptive report of what was found; in other cases, it is an attempt to elucidate the cultural history of a region; and in the best of all possible worlds, it is an explanation of how and why the people behaved the way they did.

Looking back at the larger questions addressed on Black Mesa, we realize that they have been explored in a somewhat static and isolated way. Real people do not act, consciously or unconsciously, in the rigid ways depicted here. The sense of human drama, the actual understanding of the behavior is missing. What is required is a perspective which permits an understanding of human beings acting and reacting to changing social and environmental situations both on a seasonal and long-term basis.

The studies on population and environmental change seem to indicate that the Black Mesans responded in a mechanical, almost barometric, way to changes in the climate. There are many causes for culture change, and there are usually many cultural responses available to a population in any given situation. How modern industrial nations have reacted to depletion of the world oil supply provides an example of how primitive farming societies might react to crop failures. Many options for short- and long-term replacement are explored. Trade and social networks are established or modified. Consumption is reduced. The options that are available depend on the nature of the culture and the character of the situation. The Black Mesans were not automatons, programmed to respond in a specific way to a five-degree lowering of the mean annual temperature. To understand why they reacted the way they did, it is necessary to understand Black Mesa culture as a holistic entity—as a system.

In spite of the assertions of some archaeologists, it is not possible to reconstruct a credible picture of an entire extinct culture. Not all behavior results in the material things that can be recovered by the archaeologist's trowel, brush, microscope, or backhoe. Archaeologists must realize that parts of the cultural system will never be recovered. This does not mean that we have explored the outer limits of understanding and explaining past behavior and that we cannot make our subjects of exploration more human. Refinements in technique and theory continue, sometimes barely perceptible and other times with the momentum of a grand jeté, much like the evolution of black-on-white Anasazi pottery design.

What aspects of an extinct cultural system can the archaeologist realistically expect to investigate with some degree of confidence? A glance at the chapter on Black Mesa problem spheres makes it quickly apparent that we have tended to focus on the economic system including population, and on the environment, a direct link to the ecosystem. This is not an accident of our training and intellectual interests, but rather reflects both the relative ease with which these aspects of the system can be probed and the great amount of information which can be retrieved from the investment of a finite amount of time and money.

The vast majority of the artifacts an archaeologist recovers are tools or their fragments: tools for manufacturing other tools, for producing and processing plant food and collecting animals, collecting wood and cleaning and processing hides, or making baskets. The shell bracelet or turquoise bead is the rare exception to the hundreds of manos, projectile points, and cooking vessels found.

Not only are the economically related artifacts more plentiful, but they provide a more direct link to the environment which usually can be reconstructed more easily than can the social or religious systems. Is it any wonder that most archaeologists use the ecosystem concept and tend to be intellectual Marxists, when the focus is on natural resources and on modes of production?

The primacy that archaeologists usually give to the environment and to subsistence does not mean that the sociocultural and ideological aspects of the society are ignored. As the words "cultural system" imply, a true understanding of the system means the interactions of the subsystems are as important as the subsystems themselves. The interaction of the economic, social, religious, and environmental subsystems produces an entire cultural system that is greater than the sum of its parts.

The variable functions of the great kiva provide a good example of how the archaeologist tends to view the cultural spectrum through an ecological and economic prism, while also examining the social and religious aspects of the system. The great kiva was part of the religious or ideological subsystem in that it was a structure used for ceremonial purposes. It provided a central location for people from different villages to renew and reaffirm beliefs important to the maintenance of their culture. But much like the cathedrals of medieval Europe, great kivas almost certainly served social and economic functions as well.

The bazaars, fairs, and trading booths which surrounded the cathedral on saints' days and other religious holidays attracted people from many villages over a wide area, and were probably similar to great kiva ancillary functions. As the selling of a wife in Thomas Hardy's *Mayor of Casterbridge* shows, there was a social aspect to these affairs which resulted in the chance for people to congregate, to mix genes, share pottery designs, and meet potential spouses.

The location of great kivas was determined by both the cultural and natural environment. The difficulty of communication, the specialized production of goods in various villages, the localization of various natural resources such as piñon nuts or clay, and the vagaries of abundance in some areas and scarcity in others, made it economically sensible to have periodic centralized gatherings to exchange ideas and goods. By examining the variability in the environment and in economic production, these multifunctional, intercommunity gathering places may be located. No function may be more important than any other, as in the internal combustion engine the ignition system is no less important than carburetion. Yet the archaeologist most often finds the economic and environmental systems easiest to work with for providing explanations about behavior. However, this emphasis has sometimes blinded us to the role of ideological and social spheres in explaining culture change and stability.

🐚 THE BLACK MESA BIG PICTURE

Integrating data to provide a glimpse of the Black Mesa cultural system is a herculean task, given the deluge of information, the number of specialized studies, and their sometimes conflicting results.

Diverse research efforts have demonstrated that northeastern Black Mesa was sparsely occupied by about 600 B.C., perhaps on a seasonal basis, by Basketmaker II people with a mixed agricultural and hunting and gathering economy. While population fluctuated, a general upward trend is seen, culminating in the Lamoki and Toreva phases. Some evidence indicates that the movement to the uplands away from the major drainages and year-long habitation of the region was due to a combination of increasing population and a more favorable climate. Movement to the uplands and a wetter environmental situation does not necessarily mean that there was a continuing amelioration of living conditions and increasing dependence on agriculture. Some evidence suggests that while the environmental and economic picture was generally improving, short periods of environmental degradation occurred, with a reversion to a greater reliance on hunting and gathering. By about A.D. 1150, increased population and a deteriorating environment coincided with the abandonment of northeastern Black Mesa and a retrenchment by the Anasazi into larger communities in somewhat lower and wetter localities north and south of the coal lease areas.

These are events in the culture history which are not really explained; that is, we do not truly understand why the population increased, or precisely how environmental factors work on the social, economic, and religious aspects of the society. Nor is there any real comprehension of the cultural aspects of the abandonment process.

The most successful synthesis and explanation has been made by John Ware, a field school student in the summer of 1968 who rapidly worked his way up to assistant director of the project in 1972. What follows is in large part adapted from his doctoral dissertation.

The first step in understanding the cultural dynamics of Black Mesa is to determine the nature of the subsistence system in great detail, not only for the long term as we have done, but also on a seasonal basis. This knowledge will shed light on the decisions or adaptations the people had to make in many facets of their behavior.

Subsistence activities can be divided into procurement systems or sets of tasks necessary to exploit a particular food resource: 1) collecting wild and semicultivated plants, 2) hunting large game animals, 3) hunting small game animals, 4) floodwater agriculture, and 5) rainfall agriculture. This classification is not arbitrary, but reflects distinctions made by the modern Hopi in their subsistence activities. Furthermore, these categories are relatively easy to distinguish in the archaeological record. Plant and animal remains can be recovered, and a combination of site location and ethnographic analogy to the modern Hopi can be used to reconstruct farming activities.

Since there are no *major* changes in procurement systems on Black Mesa, but rather subtle shifts in emphasis, a picture of the subsistence base can be provided which emphasizes different procurement systems for an average annual cycle.

Spring

In spring, procurement focused on the collection of wild annuals and tender leafy plants, roots, and cactus pads. Some of these plants may have been semicultivated by weeding or removing competing plants, but they were not necessarily planted. The various disturbances around dwellings in fallow fields often encouraged certain types of annuals such as chenopodium and amaranth to grow because they favor disturbed soil.

Hunters concentrated on small animals, such as rabbits and rodents, which could be caught in snares or killed with specialized hunting sticks. Later in spring, as the first tender shoots of the cultivated crops began to appear and were most susceptible to small mammals looking for anything green and juicy, there were communal hunts. These hunts involved most of the people in the community in driving the animals into narrow canyons where they could be caught in large nets, killed, and butchered.

Concurrent with the collecting of wild foods was the preparation of fields and the planting and nurturing of crops. While the broad categories of flood-watered and rainfall-watered fields are used, considerable variation is found within the two classes. Floodwater farming can be done on the floors of the larger washes. Here soil is deep, the water table high, and the flow of the stream often available to the fields before the arroyos are deeply entrenched below the surface of the arable land. These are the environmental situations where most Navajo on Black Mesa plant today. Other floodwater farming locations are at the base of hills, in natural basins, or at the edge or bottom of small arroyos (Fig. 8.1). In these areas runoff from small ephemeral rivulets, or low hills which act as watersheds, either naturally or with human aid, is diverted onto agricultural plots. Rainfall can be used directly, of course, to water fields, but in these situations, care has to be taken to ensure that the plots are in areas that are best for water retention. Floodwater farming is generally preferred because, when it rains, the crops derive benefit from direct precipitation as well as from the water diverted from watersheds.

Figure 8.1. Navajo cornfield in a sandy wash bottom. This is probably very similar to prehistoric Anasazi agricultural techniques.

The amount of effort needed to prepare the soil and to plant varied greatly depending on field location, soil conditions, and crops grown. Most of the individual fields were probably quite small, because land favorable for agriculture is scattered over the mesa in small pockets. In some years, it may have been necessary to bring water to each plant during the critical germination and early growth period of spring, usually a very dry period in the Southwest.

Summer

During the summer, the focus of wild plant procurement activities shifted from the young leafy greens to herbs and wild grass seeds as they ripened. One of the most important wild plant foods came from Indian rice grass (Fig. 8.2). The seeds are burned away from the husks and parched by being rolled and shaken in a basket containing live coals. During the growing season, the harvesting of greens and seeds shifted from the lower elevations where growth and ripening occurred earliest to the higher regions where it occurred later. Some of these collecting trips may have required overnight stays at locations away from the main habitation sites.

Hunting in summer was probably the same as in spring, with the major emphasis on smaller mammals. Occasionally a deer or other large animal might be killed.

During early summer, cultivated plants occasionally had to be hand-watered, but by mid-July and August almost daily showers provided a great deal of moisture during this optimum growing period. Little tending of the crops was required until they approached maturity, when they needed constant attention to ward off marauding birds and animals.

A modern day Pueblo delicacy is steamed green corn. Presumably, by midsummer a portion of the corn crop was sacrificed for gourmet feasting. Late in summer some fully ripened crops might be harvested and processed, especially if there was the prospect of an early killing frost. If the crops had the good fortune to survive the early dry part of the growing season, the next stress period would be the rush to maturity before the freezing evenings of late summer and early fall. The twin enemies were the lack of water and the short growing season.

Figure 8.2. Indian rice grass, whose seeds were an important wild plant food for the Anasazi

Fall

During the autumn months, wild plant procurement continued early in the season, ending with intensive piñon nut harvesting, in years when they were plentiful. Cactus fruit and juniper berries supplemented the piñon nut diet. Piñon nuts are very high in protein and fat, and remain an important cash crop to this day. Nevertheless, good nut crops are highly localized. The piñon tree seems almost ubiquitous in Anasazi country, but high-yield crops come in cycles over several years and these peak years usually vary from area to area. Therefore, it is often necessary to travel considerable distances to find an area with a good nut crop. The nuts also ripen at different times, thereby requiring harvesting at lower elevations early in the season and then in the highlands as the days get shorter.

Wild plant resources became scarcer as winter drew closer and hunting, especially of large mammals, became important. The hunting of deer becomes more productive when the bucks begin to meet up with does during the mating season, forming larger herds. Presumably much of the meat was dried and stored for consumption during periods when other food supplies were exhausted. Hunting of rabbits and rodents decreased at this time.

Early in the fall, harvesting, processing, and storage of domesticated crops required much time and effort. Corn had to be shucked and squash and beans dried, then stored in rooms and containers that were as rodent proof as possible. Seeds had to be selected and protected for planting in the spring.

If conditions during the growing season were favorable, the fall was the most bountiful and intensely active time of the year.

Winter

During the winter months, between the first and last snow (usually December through March on Black Mesa), large mammal procurement was the major subsistence activity. It would certainly be the most productive procurement strategy in terms of calories gained for energy expended. Furthermore, with snow cover large mammals would have been easier to see and hunt. Little time was spent collecting wild plant foods except for some cactus pads which can be gathered year-round.

Stored wild and domesticated foods were very important at this time of year. If part of the annual cycle of the food procurement system had failed, the effects would have been most evident in the late winter and early spring. Signs of nutritional stress in the Black Mesa skeletal remains are ample evidence that the food production and collection systems failed frequently. No one escaped the physical punishment of not having what is today called the "minimum daily requirement" of some nutritional element.

There are two important aspects of the annual procurement system which are important to understanding culture change on Black Mesa. First, availability of food and, therefore, procurement activities, vary with the seasons. Second, during most seasons the number of exploitable food resources available usually exceeds the number of resources which are actually heavily exploited. It is the old saw of the starving man in the midst of potentially life-saving foods. This seemingly bizarre situation is really a necessity and the result of decisions to emphasize certain procurement systems and to ignore or downplay others. It is an ordering of priorities that archaeologists call scheduling, which resolves conflicts within the community over the allotment of time and energy to different classes of food resources which are available simultaneously.

An example of the potential conflict in scheduling on Black Mesa exists between late summer and early fall wild grass procurement, agricultural harvesting, and the hunting of large mammals. If piñon nuts ripened early, this might also cause a scheduling conflict, especially since piñon cones were often collected before they opened and the nuts were fully mature, to beat the piñon jays and rodents to the protein-rich crop.

The scheduling conflict may not be as severe as it appears at first glance, since, despite much recent writing about male and female roles in preindustrial societies, all societies on the cultural-evolutionary ladder equivalent to the Kayenta Anasazi had a relatively rigid division of labor along sexual lines. Generalizing from ethnographic studies, we can say that almost certainly the men hunted large game and snared smaller animals. They also helped with the heavy work in the fields. The women were probably the primary garden tenders and, along with the children, collected the wild plant foods. All members probably helped in the community drives to collect small animals. While this division of labor resolved some of the scheduling conflicts, others could not be avoided.

If women were heavily involved in harvesting and collecting wild seeds and nuts, decisions had to be made about the time involvement devoted to each procurement system. These decisions were not arbitrary, but had profound cultural evolutionary considerations.

Prior to the development of an agricultural subsistence base in what was later to become the Anasazi country, later summer–early fall procurement systems were probably dominated, especially for the women and older children, by the collecting of wild grasses and nuts. This subsistence strategy influenced community size, location, and the duration of stay at any one locality. The introduction of agriculture did not change this subsistence strategy overnight, and major scheduling decisions or conflicts did not occur. The semidomesticated or domesticated crops were not high yield and were not, at first, an important element in the procurement system. No community was going to desert the relatively sure crop of wild plant foods to speculate on the commodity market in corn futures. They were, however, willing to plant or tend small patches of domesticates if it did not interfere with obtaining wild plants. If the corn or squash survived, they provided a welcome addition to the wild food supply.

As domesticated crop yields increased because of the introduction of more productive hybrids, better climatic situations, and increased knowledge about the care and feeding of domesticates, less time was devoted to harvesting wild foodstuffs. This prehistoric "green revolution," or rather, evolution, took place at the expense of the wild seed and nut procurement system. Decisions had to be made in terms of a return on investment and the amount of time allocated to a subsistence endeavor at the expense of a conflicting one. While the decisions had to be made, they were not momentous. That is, scheduling changes were gradual. Occasionally, however, a calamitous event such as the failure of a piñon crop over a large area might affect the fall scheduling of the following year.

The decision to stress one procurement system at the expense of any other, while usually gradual, radically altered many facets of the culture. It is again instructive to use the example of changes in community location, permanence, and size, as the Black Mesans scheduled more time for agriculture rather than for wild plant food collection. Scheduling for agriculture not only means decreasing dependence on the fall wild plant procurement system, but it demands that the spring and fall habitations be the same, for in order to harvest domesticates in fall, it is necessary to plant at the same place in the spring. With the decision to invest more heavily in agricultural procurement, it is advisable to maintain at least a skeleton work force near the fields during the entire growing period rather than simply during critical sowing and harvesting periods. Agriculture not only permits a more settled existence, it demands it. Furthermore, energy cost effectiveness dictates that permanent habitation sites be located near the farm land. There is also an economic advantage to larger communities in a society heavily dependent on agriculture. Agriculture demands intensive labor investment in small areas at certain times of the year. In contrast, wild seed and nut collecting, while also seasonally proscribed, is most effectively accomplished by small, scattered groups.

In the case of the Anasazi occupation of Black Mesa, we are probably not viewing an all-or-nothing situation; that is, it always was a subsistence system based on the five procurement systems described earlier. The scheduling decisions were ones of emphasis. If the yield of one procurement system was lower than expected, efforts were made to reschedule and emphasize other procurement systems. How these decisions were made will be discussed later in this chapter.

The Black Mesa cultural scene was *not* one of an inexorable march from dabbling in domesticates, with a primary reliance on wild plants and animals, to the Anasazi equivalent of agribusiness. Instead, they probably relied increasingly on agriculture (with wild swings of the pendulum) with rescheduling dependent on seasonal environmental conditions. Plant material recovered from various phases indicates that rescheduling was continually taking place.

It is therefore important to understand that scheduling has short- and long-term effects. Short-term scheduling can take place on a seasonal or even day-to-day basis and, while affecting the subsistence economy of a community to various degrees, in most instances it would not affect long-term evolutionary trends. If, on the other hand, scheduling was consistently toward an increased reliance on agricultural procurement systems, the society might become so specialized that rescheduling would be difficult or even impossible.

The ecosystem concept rules that like a plant or animal, a society that becomes too specialized, too dependent on narrowly focused procurement systems (be it a single plant species on which an animal depends or petroleum products for a society), has a more difficult time adapting in the face of change.

THE HOPI MODEL

How a society schedules in order to diversify its subsistence base rather than specialize, is exemplified by the present-day Hopi agricultural system. Individual fields are small and scattered in many diverse environments. Some fields are in low sandy depressions where water collects after a rain. Some are on the flood plain of major washes where the water table is high, or water can be diverted onto them or carried by hand to individual plants. The most productive plots are near the base of springs where an assured water supply can be channeled by short, narrow irrigation ditches to the crops. These spring-fed plots are small and usually reserved for prestige crops, such as tobacco. Plots are also situated in sand dunes which would seem to be the driest of all environments, but which are actually excellent conservators of moisture. The seeds must be planted deeply, often 8 inches or more, to obtain enough moisture to germinate. These seeds must also have the genetic characteristics which allow them to sprout through the considerable overburden of sand. Plants are also grown in the bottoms of arroyos of varying sizes. This increases the chance that some of the crops may reach maturity. If there are heavy rains, the plants in the larger arroyos will be washed out, but those in smaller arroyos will survive because they will get enough water. On the other hand, if it is a dry season with few storms, the plants in the larger washes will get sufficient water to survive, while those in the smaller cuts which carry less water will wither and die.

By taking advantage of the environmental diversity, distributing their small garden plots in many ecological niches, the Hopi are assured that some plants will not fall victim to the notorious capriciousness of the southwestern climate. In the Four Corners region thunderstorms can be so restricted in space that a small area can be inundated with a torrential downpour, while a few feet away the soil remains bone dry. This act of the gods places a premium on the diversity of farm plot locations to take advantage of the spotty climatic variation with different types of fields employing direct rainfall and floodwater agriculture.

The planting decisions regarding location and scheduling do not take place in a social and religious vacuum. Rather than individuals making specific long-range decisions about subsistence, a complex network of social institutions regulates Hopi subsistence activities. The regulatory effect of the social institutions and customs means that decisions do not have to be made for each activity. Instead, subsistence behavior is governed by social and religious custom.

While Pueblo social and religious organization is notoriously complex and varies from group to group, a simplified overview of the Hopi organizational system, the tribe closest to the coal lease area, will provide a glimpse of the intertwined relationship between social structure, religion, and environment. The systemic and interlocking nature of the Hopi cultural system is so obvious that it is often used as an example of the holistic character of culture and environment.

The Hopi do not constitute a tribe with a paramount chief. Until recently no political organization united the many Hopi villages at the southern extremity of Black Mesa. Instead, the Hopi are united by common custom and language. Each individual pueblo or town was a political entity, united by a common culture, much like Greek city states. Even this comparison tends to obscure the real nature of Hopi social organization, for the true interlocking social units are the lineages, clans, and clan clusters. As mentioned earlier, a lineage is a group of descendants of a common ancestor who recognize descent through one side of the family; in the case of the Hopi, through the female line—a matrilineage. The nuclear family, the common family type in Anglo American society, is a weak, temporary unit because married men go to live with their wives. The household usually consists of several nuclear families: married sisters, their husbands who married in, their children, and the mother of the sisters and her husband who moved in. The members of a lineage, however, usually live in the same house or contiguous group of house units. Married men live with their wives, but view the households of their mothers and sisters as their "true" homes, to which they often return for various ceremonies. One or more lineages are named clans, all members of which trace their ancestry through a mythical common ancestor, such as a crow or spider, through the female line. The oldest woman of one of the lineages is the head of the clan, and there is usually a clan ceremonial house and a special clan fetish, such as a stone and feather wrapped in a corn husk. The male clan head is the brother or maternal uncle of the female clan head rather than the husband of the female clan head, and the brother or maternal uncle is in charge of most of the clan rituals even after he has married and moved to his wife's household. Clans are ranked by prestige, the oldest clans in the village being considered most important.

Clans are clustered into larger unnamed groups which are exogamous; that is, even people within clan clusters cannot intermarry. The lineage and the clan, however, are the most significant aspects of Hopi social organization. It is the kin unit which maintains and preserves the economic goods and ceremonial rites in trust for future generations. The clan, not the individual, is the land-holding unit, and the clan controls religious ceremonies and ritual paraphernalia. The women of the clan own the houses, prepare and distribute food, and are responsible for the clan's ritual possessions. The husbands who have married into the clan work the clan's fields, teach and show warmth to their children. Men born into the clan are responsible for the discipline of their sisters' children and are responsible for much of the ceremonial activity, even after they have married and are living within their wives' households.

Hopi ceremonial activity emphasizes control of the natural environment, especially weather control. While all village members belong to the Katcina cult, the representation of a supernatural being believed to have the power to bring rain and general harmony to the Hopi, a series of ceremonial associations are controlled by clans. While individual clans are responsible for specific ceremonies, the membership of the ceremonial association crosscuts clan membership. The village is integrated on a ceremonial level, ensuring large group participation while making one group responsible for the impressive and detailed ceremony. It also ensures that competition for ceremonial power will not develop because while any individuals can be inducted into a ceremonial association, the responsibility for the ceremony is inherited through clan lines. Kivas are also owned by clans and are the focus of many ceremonial activities. Although men are the main participants in most kiva-held ceremonial functions, they, of course, inherit their kiva membership through their mother's clan.

The two most salient features of the Hopi social-economic-religious-environmental system are the interrelatedness of the parts and the ability of the system to adapt to changing environmental and demographic variables. The Hopi cultural system is a highly flexible organization which helps to maintain an equilibrium in a very diverse environment. The effects of the environment, with drought, torrential summer rains, short growing season, violent spring sandstorms, and highly localized showers, can be minimized by a social and religious organization which stresses community welfare, sharing, and cooperation. Since the clan owns the productive agricultural land and since that land is divided among many different environmental zones, such as irrigated plots, sand dunes, and arroyo bottoms, some crops are bound to reach maturity. The individual household does not have to assume the entire risk of crop failure by maintaining a single plot in one environment. Instead, the clan acts as a health insurance system by spreading the risks. This is a well known ecological principle: in diversity there is stability. The physical characteristics of humans themselves have been used as an example of this principle. While other animals can run faster, see better and smell better, our physical attributes are so generalized, so diverse, that we have not adapted to one narrow environment or to one or two characteristics of that environment. Culture, of course, has expanded our ability to adapt. Clothes allow us to live in the arctic, submarines enable us to go beneath the sea, and lunar modules make it possible to land on the earth's satellite. By not overspecializing, by spreading the risks and emphasizing cooperation, even in clan-controlled ceremonies which stress weather control, the environmental depredations can be minimized. The fact that married men return for religious ceremonies to their clan (which is determined through the female line) underscores the unity and cooperation within the clan. While the individual family may suffer, and Hopi divorce is even more common than in a typical California suburb, the clan, that important economic unit, is strengthened.

The concept of diversity enhancing stability does not mean that spreading the risks has always been a successful technique for maintaining the status quo between the harsh environment and Hopi culture. There are examples of clans dying out, communities becoming extinct, and villages absorbing outsiders into their systems. The social and religious organization described above is not an inflexible system, but rather encourages changing relationships between people in response to variations in human demography and the natural environment.

The Hopi meet subsistence stress by dispensing with the community's less prestigious lineages and clans which then go to form their own community, move into an already established village— or starve. The population can disperse without abandoning the village, for all efforts are concentrated on preserving the key clans, those that according to legend arrived first at the village. Both history and archaeology have demonstrated that when a village gets too large, it is an unstable social unit because the environment does not permit large agglomerations of people to live together for long periods of time. Colony villages are therefore established, usually by the less prestigious lineages and clans.

The stress of movement and separation on the founders of the colony villages is eased somewhat by kinship ties to the mother village. For people moving to the next village, religious and social organizations provide a ready-made niche for them. If they are of the Bear Clan, they have an established social and religious position in the Bear Clan of the village they are entering.

The interrelationship of the various aspects of Hopi culture is apparent in the major organizations of kinship, clan, clan clusters, religious societies and kivas. Each one of these organizations has its own way of maintaining and increasing social solidarity and yet each has overlapping membership, so the integration of the whole community is assured. That the Hopi cultural system has been effective in maintaining social order in a precarious environment is demonstrated by the persistence of their lifeway for many centuries. Legends, history, and archaeology underscore the general conservatism of Hopi culture and its great antiquity.

ᘓ BACK TO BLACK MESA

While there is little doubt that the prehistoric Black Mesans are the ancestors of the Hopi, great care must be exercised in making analogies. The fact that archaeologists can detect kivas in prehistoric sites, for example, does not necessarily mean that they had precisely the same function as kivas do in Hopi villages today. Form does not necessarily follow function, as is obvious when occasionally we see a toilet bowl used as a planter for flowers.

Careful use of ethnographic analogy can, nevertheless, provide valuable insight into the human behavior of the Black Mesans. Comparison to living people and the archaeological and environmental record can be used to explain the increasing sedentism and population growth on northeastern Black Mesa, the way Black Mesans distributed themselves over the landscape, and how the abandonment process worked.

The earliest occupations on Black Mesa were probably mostly seasonal. The Basketmaker II, or Lolomai phase people, were scattered in both the upland and lowland areas near the washes. While the corn in the Lolomai phase is the same type and theoretically of equal productivity as the corn found in the latest Black Mesa sites, there are certain indications that the earliest Black Mesans were not as dependent on domesticated crops as were later settlers. The fact that Lolomai phase sites are located in diverse environments may mean that there was not intense specialization focused on only a few procurement systems and that domesticated crops were not as important as in later periods. Furthermore, beans, that vital source of protein, were not cultivated by the Black Mesa Anasazi until Basketmaker III times.

While it is possible for humans to live without starch, as do Eskimo groups who live on a diet consisting almost entirely of meat, it is impossible to survive without protein. Corn provides several essential amino acids, but starch crops cannot form the exclusive subsistence base of a people. Since no animals (except for the dog and turkey) were domesticated and no protein crops were grown prior to Basketmaker III, the essential protein and fat had to come from wild animals and piñon nuts. Hunting and collecting is most efficiently done by dispersed populations. Intensified agriculture of starch crops would not solve the problem. Small groups scattered over the landscape would most effectively obtain the needed fat and protein. These facts almost assured small, widely dispersed communities or residential mobility.

Like corn, beans were introduced from Mexico. They are a hardy crop, requiring little water, can be easily stored for long periods, and require little preparation; they do, nevertheless, require much attention during the entire growing period, unlike corn, which can be left for long periods of time. Adding protein and fat-rich beans to the starchy corn made for a balanced domesticated plant diet, permitted the aggregation of larger groups of people, and reduced reliance on hunting and gathering; it also forces scheduling decisions and increases specialization, thereby reducing adaptability according to the rule that diversity increases stability.

The Black Mesans' choice to favor domesticated crops at the expense of hunting and gathering neatly illustrates how trends toward specialization reduce stability. Domesticates tend to require similar environmental conditions, a long growing season, water at critical periods, and so on. A bumper crop of piñons, rabbits, or deer, which tends to increase and decrease in several-year cycles, depends on climatic variables different from the ones that affect annual crops. The fortuitous coincidence of a bad corn harvest and a bountiful piñon crop and deer population are much more likely to happen than a bad corn crop and a good bean harvest. The dependence on the trinity of corn, beans, and squash does not mean the people could not revert to a collecting and hunting strategy, but as we shall see, it was done at the expense of social cohesion; Black Mesa could not support many people who only foraged for a living.

The dearth of Basketmaker III or Dot Klish and slightly later phase sites in the coal lease area may be a direct result of wildly fluctuating climatic changes, with numerous dry periods culminating in a major drought about A.D. 850 to 900. The low population in the lease area during this time does not necessarily mean an unusual amount of subsistence stress, or even a great shift of populations. These early populations are represented by sites immediately off the mesa to the north and in the lower but better-watered regions only a few miles to the south and east on Black Mesa. If Shirley Powell is correct that all, or almost all of the early sites are really temporary farming, collecting, or hunting sites, all that the low density means is that the people went elsewhere for their seasonal activities. This was easy to do because the population was relatively small and the carrying capacity of the land had not been reached. People could afford to avoid the higher area with fewer springs now known as the Peabody Coal lease area.

With the concomitant growth of population and the improved environment after A.D. 900, people began to use the coal lease area with greater frequency, even to the point of establishing settlements. Most of these early settlers, logically enough, used the most productive land near the major washes where the soil is deep and the water table is relatively close to the surface. Not only was water available much of the year for crops being grown on the flood plain, but water for domestic use did not have to be carried long distances. The uplands were used for hunting and gathering and almost certainly for dry-farming as well.

The more balanced diet, improving environmental conditions, and critical scheduling decisions all had important implications for population density. Not only did improved agricultural conditions and increased yields reduce infant mortality and increase life span, but this greater population demanded intensification of agriculture.

At the same time that population expanded, so too did the amount of prime agricultural land because the ameliorating climate opened up for farming previously marginal lands. The question is did population expand because of the increase in arable land, or was the contemporaneity of expanding agricultural land and population a coincidence? These searches for "causes" emphasize the interrelatedness of the variables. The biological aspects of reproduction and nutrition in conjunction with a more favorable environmental situation and scheduling decisions were probably all mutually reinforcing.

Rapid population growth, increased utilization of the uplands, and more permanent settlement of the coal lease area were accomplished in a social and religious matrix which cushioned the impact of the changes.

It is in this situation that the Hopi culture model provides an example of how Black Mesans responded to an increasing population. While Hopi villages may have hundreds of inhabitants, many lineages, clans, and kivas, even the largest northern Black Mesa sites probably consisted of no more than 25 or 30 people, one or two lineages, and a single kiva. While there are thousands of sites in the coal lease area, they are small and scattered.

This pattern of settlement is dictated by the natural environment and the subsistence base. The Hopi can live in relatively large villages because of the constant supply of water at the southern fringes of Black Mesa and the concentration in that region of relatively good agricultural land. The situation on northern Black Mesa is quite different. Good agricultural land is spread in narrow ribbons of flood plain along the larger washes, but since the coal lease area is near the source of the washes, the flood plains there are quite narrow. The best potential agricultural plots in the uplands are in the sage-filled flats and basins where water drains after a rain and the soil is fairly deep. While this type of environment is fairly common, the size of these potential agricultural zones is small. As a result, small scattered settlements are the most efficient settlement types to exploit these environmental niches.

With an expanding population putting more land under cultivation, it makes economic sense to disperse the inhabitants so they can be close to their fields. The social mechanism by which this was done was probably by fission, as for the modern Hopi; that is, segments of lineages or sometimes even entire lineages moved from the mother community and established daughter villages. The continued relationship between Hopi mother and daughter communities reduces feelings of alienation and separation which would also have been effective in an expanding prehistoric Black Mesa population.

Thus, daughter villages were related to the mother community by kinship, economic, and religious ties. The daughter sites do not have kivas, which means that many of the most important ceremonial functions required a return to the mother community.

Furthermore, it was a means of bringing the men born into the lineage back to the original settlement, thereby reinforcing the kin ties through ceremonial means. During this period of burgeoning population and expansion into the uplands the clan and clan cluster system may have evolved, for the clan and clan clusters are one more way of reinforcing social, economic, and religious ties.

Economic stability was probably enhanced by sharing the harvest along kinship lines, as with the Hopi. Since mother and daughter settlements were using many different environments, the rule of diversity increasing stability comes into play. Two or three interrelated communities would help ensure that more varied environmental niches would be used, and kin ties would regulate the sharing of the harvest. The cliff dwelling called Standing Fall House and one or two other sites which seem to have as their sole purpose food storage and processing may have been collection and redistribution centers.

By using the Hopi model and viewing Black Mesa culture as a highly integrated system, it is possible not only to better understand the social mechanisms by which population expansion was facilitated, but also the abandonment process.

The abandonment of northeastern Black Mesa by A.D. 1150 was certainly not an event which took place because of some environmental catastrophe in a previously idyllic and stable cultural and demographic situation. That there were periods of subsistence stress and population pressure on the environment throughout the occupation is evident from the dietary deficiency apparent in the skeletons, the occasional necessity to emphasize hunting and collecting, and population movements within the lease area. The paleoclimatic evidence does indicate that a somewhat drier climatic episode was the triggering mechanism which resulted in the rapid movement of people from northeastern Black Mesa.

As was mentioned earlier, the people apparently did not need to move far. Movement to the north off Black Mesa and to the central and southern parts of the mesa put the people in the precise locations where population was concentrated during Basketmaker III and Pueblo I times, before the big population expansion throughout the Anasazi region.

However, the Klethla phase communities (ca. A.D. 1150 to 1250), were much bigger than earlier villages and were obviously amalgamations of a number of earlier communities. The concentration of population into larger settlements was probably dictated by the localization of a vital resource—water. Many Klethla and later Tsegi phase sites are situated near still flowing springs. While in previous decades relatively abundant rainfall and isolated patches of farmland had made a dispersed population attractive, a few localized but assured sources of water during the Klethla and Tsegi phases made population concentrations advisable.

The trauma of abandonment and the concerns of moving into new and larger villages were eased by the same social and religious factors which helped mitigate the strain of fissioning off population to start new daughter communities. Kin ties, clan affiliation, clan clusters, and kiva religious associations all ensured that new lineages moving into the larger village would have a specific social, economic, and religious position in an established system. The system meant that early arrivals and latecomers to the community did not have to start out life anew in an unfamiliar cultural system, but had an already established set of relationships that were dictated by custom. The dearth of whole artifacts, even such heavy items as metates, in the final phase of occupation on northeastern Black Mesa indicates that the people took everything with them because they knew where they were going and it was only a short distance. The tree-ring studies of the large cliff dwelling of Betatakin show how these large pueblos grew. Whole lineages apparently moved into these niches in the cliffs, adding their clusters of rooms to the growing bulk of the pueblo. The amalgamation of clans and kiva societies as well as simply numbers of people is also demonstrated by the presence of multiple kivas at a single site. While to the archaeologist these population movements seem quite dramatic, they were probably undertaken with little stress or strain. The adaptation to new communities and new environments was buffered by a culture which had proved its flexibility.

So ends this tale of the archaeology of Black Mesa and the prism through which we can see the component parts of a modern archaeological project. While the Black Mesa Archaeological Project has ended, work does not. Research is ongoing, new questions are being posed, and different answers to old questions are being phrased. A basic question, however, has not been addressed: what is the intellectual or social value of the countless hours, dollars, and mental gyrations that thirteen years of intense study have produced? How does the project stack up as a case study of the tenets of the "new" archaeology? The question can be answered on various levels, but no one answer is really satisfactory to everybody.

On the simplest, yet most specific level, studies such as the BMAP are just that—a slice of human prehistory in an out-of-the-way spot that happens to have coal under the surface. On this level, Black Mesa culture history is a segment of the human record, important in and of itself, as a unique and irreplaceable part of the past, unrecorded by written documentation. For many people, including most archaeologists, this simple explanation is not sufficient.

At the opposite end of the spectrum are those archaeologists who see archaeology providing the basis for constructing laws of human behavior based on the evidence of millions of years of human cultural evolution. Only archaeology, they say, can produce the data to answer questions of long-term change. During the 1960s and early 1970s, with the students' call for "relevance," lessons from archaeology even were being touted as solutions for the problems of the ghettos! Black Mesa research results do not have that potential, and probably neither does any other archaeological project, except in the most general way.

The lessons most pertinent and the values most apparent from a long-term study of an area such as Black Mesa are subtle, not awe inspiring, and really quite basic.

Physical and cultural survival depends upon adaptability, cooperation, and understanding the interrelatedness of the parts of a cultural system and the environment. Problems of declining natural resources and industrial productivity cannot be addressed in economic or political terms alone. The entire cultural matrix in which these problems are embedded must be understood, for the manipulation of one facet of a system inevitably results in changes throughout the system.

Both the uniqueness of the Black Mesa research results and the understanding of the commonalities these people shared with other culture systems provoked an awe of the extinct and a lesson for the future.

Without contract archaeology many seemingly mundane peripheral areas such as Black Mesa probably would never have been studied systematically by archaeologists. The only archaeology ever done in the coal lease area was the site that was excavated by the Rainbow Bridge Monument expedition in 1936, and it is significant that the site they excavated was unusually large. It suited their purpose because the trash midden was deep and provided information which helped to build the ceramic design evolutionary sequence for the Kayenta Anasazi. This early work helped establish a chronology for the region which BMAP was able to use as a foundation to understand the culture history of Black Mesa.

It was, however, the fortuitous circumstances of new methodological and theoretical trends combined with funds from Peabody Coal Company which permitted us to undertake a consideration of how people behaved and interacted with their environment. The detail with which the environment and the past extinct culture has to be reconstructed requires an enormous expenditure of effort and funds—far more than can be supplied by government funding agencies such as the National Science Foundation or the National Endowment for the Humanities. Only the partnership between industry, in this case the world's largest coal mining company, and academia could provide the quality and quantity of data, probably unparalleled for detail in the world, which allow us to answer the questions we have posed.

Not all of BMAP's studies have resulted in success, of course, for that is not how science works. But when one avenue of investigation failed we were able to fund another study until the numerous small studies, like building blocks, were able to be integrated, supporting one another to create an edifice we know as the Black Mesa Anasazi.

Some professional archaeologists have denigrated contract archaeology and often with good reason. Funds have been misused. Research results have not always been published. Sometimes, after the expenditure of massive amounts of money, funding agencies or firms have found the archaeology has been of such poor quality that the federal employees overseeing the work will not grant permission to proceed with the construction project.

Nevertheless, the contract situation has offered unparalleled opportunities for archaeologists to test their theories. Those opportunities must be addressed in a scientific, yet businesslike, fashion—or archaeology will become as extinct as the societies it studies.

Recommended Readings

Chapter 1

KING, THOMAS F., PATRICIA PARKER HICKMAN, AND GARY BERG
1977 *Anthropology in Historic Preservation: Caring for Culture's Clutter.* Academic Press, New York.

RATHJE, WILLIAM L., AND MICHAEL B. SCHIFFER
1982 *Archaeology.* Harcourt Brace Jovanovich, New York.

SCHIFFER, MICHAEL B., AND GEORGE J. GUMERMAN (editors)
1977 *Conservation Archaeology: A Guide for Cultural Resource Management Studies.* Academic Press, New York.

Chapter 2

GAEDE, MARC, AND MARNIE GAEDE (editors)
1980 *Camera, Spade, and Pen: An Inside View of Southwestern Archaeology.* University of Arizona Press, Tucson.

MARTIN, PAUL S., AND FRED PLOG
1973 *The Archaeology of Arizona: A Study of the Southwest Region.* Doubleday/Natural History Press, Garden City, New York.

Chapter 3

POWELL, SHIRLEY, PETER P. ANDREWS, DEBORAH L. NICHOLS, AND F.E. SMILEY
1983 Fifteen Years on the Rock: Archaeological Research, Administration, and Compliance on Black Mesa, Arizona. *American Antiquity* 48:228–252.

Chapter 4

FAGAN, BRIAN M.
1981 *In the Beginning: An Introduction to Archaeology* (4th edition). Little, Brown, Boston.

RATHJE, WILLIAM L., AND MICHAEL B. SCHIFFER
1982 *Archaeology*. Harcourt Brace Jovanovich, New York.

SHARER, ROBERT J., AND WENDY ASHMORE
1979 *Fundamentals of Archaeology*. Benjamin/Cummings, Menlo Park.

THOMAS, DAVID H.
1979 *Archaeology*. Holt, Rinehart and Winston, New York.

Chapters 5 and 6

GUMERMAN, GEORGE J., AND ROBERT C. EULER (editors)
1976 *Papers on the Archaeology of Black Mesa*. Southern Illinois University Press, Carbondale.

GUMERMAN, GEORGE J., DEBORAH WESTFALL, AND CAROL S. WEED
1972 *Black Mesa: Archaeology Investigations on Black Mesa, the 1969–1970 Seasons*. Prescott College Press, Prescott, Arizona.

POWELL, SHIRLEY
1983 *Mobility and Adaptation: The Anasazi of Black Mesa, Arizona*. Southern Illinois University Press, Carbondale.

SMILEY, F.E., DEBORAH L. NICHOLS, AND PETER P. ANDREWS (editors)
1983 *Excavations on Black Mesa, 1981: A Descriptive Report*. Center for Archaeological Investigations, Research Paper No. 36, Southern Illinois University, Carbondale.

Chapter 7

EULER, ROBERT C., GEORGE J. GUMERMAN, THOR N.V. KARLSTROM, JEFFREY S. DEAN, AND RICHARD H. HEVLY

1979 The Colorado Plateaus: Cultural Dynamics and Paleoenvironment. *Science* 205:1089–1101.

FORD, RICHARD I.
1979 Paleoethnobotany in American Archaeology. In *Advances in Archaeological Method and Theory*, vol. 2, edited by Michael B. Schiffer, pp. 285–336. Academic Press, New York.

HASSAN, FEKRI A.
1981 *Demographic Archaeology*. Academic Press, New York.

KUNITZ, STEPHEN, AND ROBERT C. EULER
1972 *Aspects of Southwestern Paleoepidemiology*. Prescott College Anthropological Reports, no. 2, Prescott College, Prescott, Arizona.

LYMAN, R. LEE
1982 Archaeofaunas and Subsistence Studies. In *Advances in Archaeological Method and Theory*, vol. 5, edited by Michael B. Schiffer, pp. 331–393. Academic Press, New York.

Chapter 8

CONNELLY, JOHN C.
1979 Hopi Social Organization. In *Southwest*, edited by Alfonso Ortiz, pp. 539–553. *Handbook of North American Indians*, vol. 9, William C. Sturtevant, general editor. Smithsonian Institution, Washington, D.C.

EGGAN, FRED
1950 *Social Organization of the Western Pueblos*. University of Chicago Press, Chicago. (Reprinted in 1970).

FRIGOUT, ARLETTE
1979 Hopi Ceremonial Organization. In *Southwest*, edited by Alfonso Ortiz, pp. 564–576. *Handbook of North American Indians*, vol. 9, William C. Sturtevant, general editor. Smithsonian Institution, Washington, D.C.

KENNARD, EDWARD A.
1979 Hopi Economy and Subsistence. In *Southwest*, edited by Alfonso Ortiz, pp. 554–563. *Handbook of North American Indians*, vol. 9, William C. Sturtevant, general editor. Smithsonian Institution, Washington, D.C.

Index

26, 105, 117, 171; seasonal round, 27–30. *See also* Southern Illinois University
Bow and arrow, 36, 62, 64
Bureau of Indian Affairs, 28
Burials, 119, 124–25. *See also* Mortuary customs

Camp fever, 25
Carbon 14 dating. *See* Dating
Carrying capacity concept, 136
Catlin, Mark, 97, 100
Cemeteries. *See* Mortuary customs
Ceramics, 37–39; Basketmaker III, 36, 64, 65; Basketmaker III–Pueblo I, 70; and exchange, 101; function, 88–89; introduction of, 64, 65; Late Pueblo II, 101–4; manufacturing, 65–66, 79; neutron activation analysis, 101–2; Pueblo I, 72, 73; Pueblo I–II, 78–80; Pueblo II, 79; Pueblo IV, 66, 114–15; and social organization, 96–97; sources, 101; thin-section analysis of, 101; typology, 39
Ceremonialism (Hopi), 162–63
Chaco Canyon, 119
Chaco tradition, 39, 84, 111
Chandler, Susan, 75
Chronology. *See* Anasazi, chronology; Dating
Cibola Gray ware, 39
Cibola White ware, 39
Classification, 16, 34–37. *See also* Ceramics, typology
Clay. *See* Ceramics; Dating, archaeomagnetic
Clemen, Bob, 95–96
Climate, 78, 90; pollen analysis of, 131–32; reconstructing past climates, 128–29, 169; tree-ring analysis of, 129–30. *See also* Black Mesa, environment of
Coal artifacts, 66

Coal mining (surface): effects on archaeology, 3; on Indian reservations, 5, 28; prehistoric, 65–66
Colorado Plateau, 53–55
Contract archaeology, 9–14; definition of, 9; federal regulations, 28–29; funding for, 9, 11–12, 172–73; reports, 12; results of, 3, 172; rise of, 9. *See also* Cultural resource management
Coprolites (feces). *See* Diet
Corn (maize). *See* Subsistence
Coronado, 115
Cradle boards, 71
Cultural ecology: definition of, 10; and environment, 127
Cultural resource management, 12–13
Cultural sequence. *See* Anasazi, chronology; Dating
Culture history, 26, 171

Danson, Ned, 20
Dating, 16–17, 40–44, 117; archaeomagnetic, 43; by association, 42; calendric dates, 17, 40; radiocarbon (C14), 17, 42–43, 58; relative, 16, 40, 74–75; stratigraphy, 16, 40; tree-ring (dendrochronology), 17, 40–42, 78, 112. *See also* Pecos Classification
Dead Juniper Wash, 133–34
Dean, Jeff, 112, 134
Demography. *See* Population
Dendrochronology. *See* Dating, tree-ring
Desha Complex, 57, 58
Deutchmann, Haree, 101
Diet: Early Pueblo II, 90, 92; reconstruction using coprolites, 90; reconstruction using skeletons, 125–27, 169. *See also* Subsistence

Kayenta tradition, 39, 56, 84. *See also* Desha Complex
Kidder, Alfred Vincent, 7, 8, 16
Kiet Siel, 112, 114
King, Jeff, 66
Kivas. *See* Architecture
Klesert, Anthony, 74, 91
Klethla phase. *See* Early Pueblo III

Lamoki phase. *See* Early Pueblo II
Late Pueblo II (Toreva), 93–104
Late Pueblo III (Tsegi), 112–14, 170
Layhe, Bob, 123–24
Lerner, Shereen, 88
Lino Black-on-gray, 70
Lino Gray, 70
Lithics: Archaic, 56–57; Basketmaker II, 58; Basketmaker III, 36; Basketmaker III–Pueblo I, 68; Pueblo I, 73; Pueblo I–II, 78; sources, 78, 98–99, 101
Lolomai phase. *See* Basketmaker II

Maize. *See* Subsistence
Martin, Debbie, 125
Martin, Paul S., 8
Mesa Verde Gray ware, 39
Mesa Verde tradition, 39, 84
Mesa Verde White ware, 39
Mesoamerican contact, 58, 65
Mogollon: first identified, 8; and Mexico, 58; and Pueblo I–II, 83
Mortuary customs, 119; Pueblo I–II, 82–83

National Heritage, Conservation and Recreation Service, 28–29
National Park Service, 28
National Register of Historic Places, 28–29
Navajo: on Black Mesa, 115; chronology, 104; model, 34, 80, 138, 153; sites surveyed, 46; Tribe and reservation, 5, 20, 28, 29
Navajo National Monument, 112
New archaeology, 17, 171
Nutrition. *See* Diet

Paleoclimate. *See* Climate
Peabody Coal Company: compliance, 27, 29; role in BMAP, 3, 5, 19, 20, 21, 22, 46, 172. *See also* Coal mining; Contract archaeology
Pecos Classification, 17, 36, 56
Pecos Ruin, 7
Phillips, Dave, 95
Pinto Complex, 57
Pithouses. *See* Architecture
Plant foods. *See* Subsistence
Plog, Steve, 26, 104
Political organization (Hopi), 161–62
Pollen, 144
Population: abandonment, 106; change, 26, 71, 72, 77, 117, 118–27, 149, 151–52, 164; estimates, 119–20; maximums, 84, 93; pressure during Late Pueblo II, 95; size, 86, 118–24; studies on Black Mesa, 120–27. *See also* Disease; Settlement pattern

Survey. *See* Field methods
Swedlund, Al, 120

Tallahogan phase. *See* Basket-
   maker III–Pueblo I
Time-space framework. *See* Classi-
   fication
Toreva phase. *See* late Pueblo II
Trade: Basketmaker III, 67–68;
   Late Pueblo II, 101; Pueblo I,
   77; Pueblo I–II, 83; Pueblo IV,
   114
Tree-ring dating. *See* Dating
Tsegi Canyon, 112, 114
Tsegi Orange ware, 101
Tsegi phase. *See* Late Pueblo III
Tusayan Corrugated, 79
Tusayan Gray ware, 39
Tusayan White ware, 39
Typology. *See* Classification

Vegetation. *See* Black Mesa, environment of
Virgin tradition, 84

Ware, John, 152
Wares. *See* Ceramics
Warfare, 106–7
Water. *See* Black Mesa, environ-
   ment of
Wepo phase. *See* Pueblo I–II
White Dog Cave, 59, 61
White Mountains, 8, 109
Winslow tradition, 84

Zuni pueblo, 115